CERTAIN TO WIN

DEAR ALEX,

I HOPE YOU
GET A CHANCE TO
READ THIS.

BEST REGARDS,

Lucok

CERTAIN TO WIN

The Strategy of John Boyd,

Applied to Business

Chet Richards

The author would like to express appreciation to Mary Boyd Holton, executrix
of the John R. Boyd estate, for permission to quote from copyrighted material.

Library of Congress Number:		2004092495
ISBN:	Hardcover	1-4134-5377-5
	Softcover	1-4134-5376-7

This book was printed in the United States of America.

To order additional copies of this book, contact:
Xlibris Corporation
1-888-795-4274
www.Xlibris.com
Orders@Xlibris.com
24705

CONTENTS

DEDICATION

To the late John Boyd, who encouraged me to start this project.
To my wife, Ginger Richards, who saw to it that I finished.
And to the late LTC Grover C. Richards, US Army,
survivor of Bataan, commander of US cavalrymen,
toughest guy I ever met, and a hell of a father.

PREFACE

If a general who heeds my strategy is employed, he is certain to win.
Sun Tzu[1]

In 2002, the major airlines of the United States lost $8.6 billion, on top of the $10.3 billion they had lost in 2001.[2] Six of the seven largest airlines also engaged in such practices as charging business travelers ten times the fares they charged vacationers, imposing $100 "change" fees, and requiring immediate rebooking in case of a change (or the traveler lost the entire amount.)

One major airline made money in 2002 and one airline did not engage in any of these egregious practices. Both airlines are, of course, the same company: Southwest Airlines. If you give people reasons to avoid your products and services, while a competitor does not, people will quit buying yours, or at least buy less of them. Now the critical question of strategy is that if I can see this and you can see it, what was the problem with the people who ran the other six airlines?

Starting in the mid-1970s, an obscure retired Air Force colonel, John R. Boyd, wondered the same thing about armies. In Vietnam, for example, we stuck with the same policies and strategies for nearly 10 years, up to when the last US personnel had to be evacuated by helicopter from the roof of our embassy in Saigon. Similarly, Boyd noted, at the start of World War II, the French and British were using the same outmoded strategies that had caused horrendous bloodbaths during World War I. The Germans, on the other hand, had developed the Blitzkrieg, and they sliced through the allied lines in a couple of weeks.

After considerable research, Boyd concluded that a small set of principles formed the foundation for the German victory and that they were primarily cultural, that is, they dealt with the behavior of people in groups. These "principles of the Blitzkrieg" do not give instructions on how to deploy tanks on the battlefield. Rather they aim to attack the ability of the other side to make effective decisions under conditions of danger, fear, and uncertainty and to increase our ability to function well under these same conditions. There was, in other words, little exclusively military about Boyd's philosophy of conflict.

Over Christmas vacation in 1987, after Boyd had completed the bulk of his work, I happened upon Tom Peters' *Thriving on Chaos*. It struck me that Peters could have modeled his organizational climate and culture after Boyd's. Moreover, Peters insisted that his recommendations enabled companies to reach decisions quickly, which was a point Boyd had been briefing around the Pentagon for the last 10 years. Although Peters did not mention Boyd by name, their conclusions were too similar to be simple coincidence.

I called Boyd and told him that he had to read Peter's book. He did, and that led him to the Toyota Production System and the works of the creators of that system, particularly Shigeo Shingo and Taiichi Ohno, and to the papers just published by researchers from the International Motor Vehicle Program underway at MIT to see if the Japanese did build better cars cheaper, or whether they were dumping them at below cost into the US market.

The upshot of all this was that Boyd concluded that the Toyota Production System was another implementation of the principles he had associated with the Blitzkrieg. As odd as this may seem—a doctrine of war and a car manufacturing system turning out to be brothers under the skin—they both use time as their principle strategic device, their organizational climates share several elements, and they both trace back to the school of strategy whose earliest known documentation is Sun Tzu's *The Art of War*.

Peters later wrote me that he had indeed read about Boyd's work in James Fallows' 1982 book, *National Defense*, but had overlooked it in the details of preparing references for his book. Boyd and Peters did meet on one occasion, and Peters featured Boyd in a column, calling the OODA loop "the real nub of competitiveness." Boyd also appears several times in Peters' latest book, *Re-imagine!* At about the time Peters was finishing *Re-imagine!* incidentally, US Marines on the other side of the world were debating how they would use Boyd and the OODA loop in the final assault on Baghdad.[3]

My plan in this book is to introduce Boyd's philosophy of conflict, for which I'll use the term "maneuver conflict," by examining how it works in the two primary areas where it has been applied: in armed conflict as maneuver warfare and in manufacturing as the Toyota Production System, or as it is more widely known, "lean production."[4] This is a technique Boyd called "many sided, implicit cross referencing," which means to slice the problem a number of ways, draw ideas from across a range of disciplines, and see if we can discern common patterns.

The principles of maneuver conflict not only explain why the managers of the largest US airlines are running their companies into the ground, they also prescribe solutions. Southwest Airlines, the one consistently profitable major, operates more according to the principles of maneuver conflict than does its competitors, although I have no idea whether Herb Kelleher and the other creators of their system ever heard the term or studied any of its concepts. It would not be too far-fetched, since the military, particularly the Marine Corps, has adopted elements of maneuver warfare since the mid-1980s, and there are many ex-service members working at the airlines.

This book began in 1988 from a briefing on maneuver warfare and business. Boyd read, commented on, and corrected every draft until his death in 1997. The chapters on climate and strategy are very similar to the last manuscript Boyd saw, although I have updated the examples and changed a few "buts" to "however." I have also had the opportunity to re-read his exegesis of strategy, *Patterns of Conflict*, a few more times, discuss it with his other surviving colleagues, and present it to military and commercial audiences.

Many thanks also to the people without whose support this book would not have happened: Col Mike Wyly, USMC (ret.), Boyd's co-conspirator in installing maneuver warfare as Marine Corps doctrine, who read several drafts and kept me out of trouble when I ventured into maneuver warfare; Col G. I. Wilson, USMCR, co-originator of the concept of "fourth generation warfare," whose insights on applying Boyd to business made a difference early on; Chuck Spinney, Boyd acolyte and Pentagon insider, who told me that for Boyd's ideas to grow, they had to reach people outside of the military; Robert Coram, author of *Boyd, The Fighter Pilot Who Changed the Art of War*, who insisted I resurrect the manuscript and read all the drafts after Boyd; Jeannine Addams, owner of Tarkenton & Addams, the only PR agency in the world run according to Boyd, who patiently made time in her busy days to read and discuss awkward passages and who took my photo for the cover; Dr. Linda Beckerman, colleague at Lockheed, who was present at the creation and has applied many of these ideas to the form of conflict known as project management; Mickey Pittman, founder and president of Lead the Way, Inc., who read the manuscript and contributed his insights from the viewpoint of the special operator; Lane Desborough of Honeywell, who gave the manuscript its final editing and sanity check; Kristin Wohlleben, of Tarkenton & Addams, who lent her design magic to the project; and my wife, Ginger Richards, who suffered not always patiently through the many drafts, and also selected the interior layouts and designed the cover.

Chet Richards
Atlanta, Georgia
March 2004

CHAPTER I

Nor the Battle to the Strong

The race is not to the swift, nor the battle to the strong, neither yet bread to the wise, nor yet riches to men of understanding, nor yet favor to men of skill; but time and chance happeneth to them all.
Ecclesiastes, IX, 1

Why Study War?

"Much strategy," ancient commentators wrote, "triumphs over little."[5] You would be hard put to demonstrate this by looking at business strategy today. That phrase can mean almost anything, from techniques for running the business itself, such as in "a strategy of outsourcing," to comforting aphorisms about teamwork, to mystical pronouncements on vision. Even if we grant that it means something, "strategy" seems lost in the other prescriptions for success in business, which today seem focused on ways to lower costs or respond faster to customer needs. Few writers today are willing to proclaim strategy as the primary key to success.

However, few also would argue its power in other areas, such as war. It is not unknown in war, for example, for a side to win every battle, but through flawed strategy to lose the war. This is one view of what happened to the United States in Vietnam. There is a school of strategy—it forms the ultimate foundation for this book—which teaches that the best strategy wins without ever engaging in battle at all.

One problem may be that some who study military strategy fail to deal with the nature of business, with its multiplicity of competitors, legal requirements such as detailed financial reporting, loose definition of "victory," and most frustrating, the impossibility of attacking competitors directly. Such misconceptions have led to the claim that although strategy is fine for war, it has little to do with the problems of running a business.

I propose to resurrect business strategy by returning to a form of conflict that is simpler in the abstract, war.[6] Businesses will not be able to use the specific tactics, principles, or strategies of war since these are designed to destroy adversaries—morally and mentally if possible, physically if necessary—and not to attract customers. War strategies, however, rest on a deeper foundation of people working together under stress and uncertainty, and good ones shape the terms of the conflict to their liking before combat begins. Such an environment describes modern business, and strategies based on this foundation will work as well for business as for war.

To illustrate the elemental power of strategy, let's look at one of the most spectacular triumphs in the history of warfare.

The Blitzkrieg

During the night of May 9th and 10th, 1940, Germany attacked Belgium and Holland. (Maps 1 and 2)

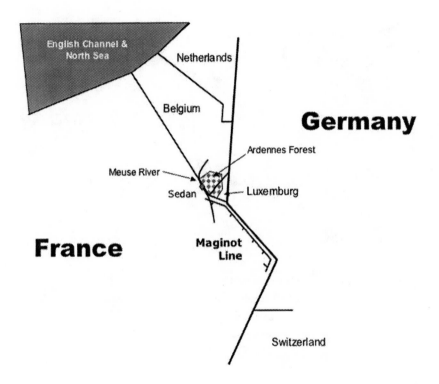

Map 1—Western Front, May 1940

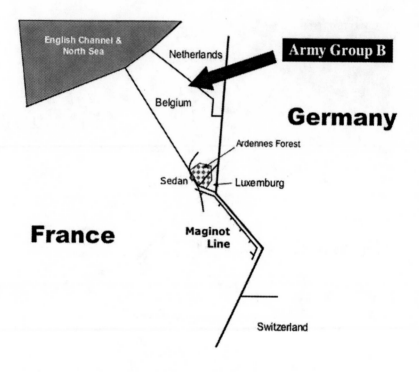

Map 2—The Attack Begins

The French and their British allies had anticipated the attack, which was similar to how the Germans had started World War I a generation earlier, and they rushed forward to meet them. The idea was that when the trenches formed, as the allies believed they must, as they had in every war since the US Civil War, they would form outside the borders of France. (Map 3)

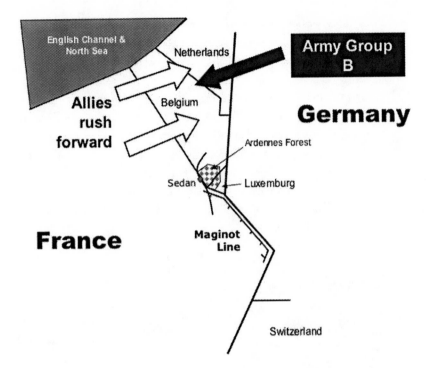

Map 3—The Allies Respond

It was a trap. It was as if the Germans had not only read the Allies' minds, but were planting thoughts in them as well. Everything the Germans did was designed to reinforce the Allied conclusion that the main thrust was coming through the flat terrain of the Low Countries—military eyes recognized it as good tank country and tank warfare was known to be a German forte. German deception succeeded to the extent that ten days later, as the real German main thrust was approaching the French coast miles to the west, Churchill was still reassuring the English people that events were under control:

> *It would be foolish, however, to disguise the gravity of the hour. It would be still more foolish to lose heart and courage or to suppose that well-trained, well-equipped armies numbering three or four millions of men can be*

overcome in the space of a few weeks, or even months, by a scoop, or raid of mechanized vehicles, however formidable. We may look with confidence to the stabilization of the Front in France... May 19, 1940

As Churchill was soon to realize—barely in time to order the withdrawal of the surviving British forces from Dunkirk—the German penetration was far more than a "scoop or raid." Three corps composed of eight German armored divisions, "Panzers,"[7] had snaked through narrow roads in the dense Ardennes Forest in southern Belgium and Luxembourg. By the morning of May 14, they were across the Meuse River at Sedan and began streaming into France. One week later, they reached the sea. (Map 4)

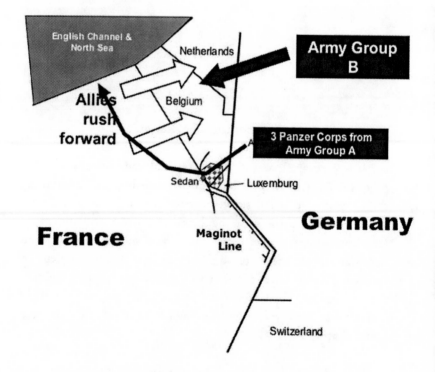

Map 4—The Trap Closes

A spectacular military feat, but why should a manager or anybody in business during the early 21st century care? True, the German victory in France led to five more years of war in Europe, the Holocaust and the deaths of tens of millions of other civilians, and the eventual triumph of the Soviet Union, the Cold War, and 50 years of Stalinist repression. This was unspeakably tragic, but there is nothing any of us can do about it now. There is, however, one good reason for looking over the shoulders of Hitler and his generals, as repugnant as we find their aims and ideology. At the start of the attack on France, the Germans had no advantage in numbers and lagged in technology. Yet they won and won easily, and they did it through the application of strategy. *Their strategy was so powerful that in one two-week period, it set aside 300 years of military history.*

If we as owners and employees of commercial enterprises could conjure up and harness even a fraction of the power of the German strategy, perhaps we could avoid the ills that befell Enron, WorldCom, the largest airlines, and so much of the economy and run our businesses more profitably over a longer period of time.

Such a scheme is possible and many of today's most successful companies, from Dell Computer to Toyota to Southwest Airlines, use strategies that at their cores tap into the same source of advantage that the Germans discovered. The late US Air Force Colonel John R. Boyd[8] provided the best description of this source in terms that apply to any form of competition between thinking beings—business certainly fits this definition—and his concepts have been adopted as doctrine by no less than the US Marine Corps, the finest military service on the planet today.[9]

We will mine the Blitzkrieg further to find the essence of the German strategy.

Should France and Britain Have Won?

Although France was still recovering from World War I, she was well aware of the threat to the east. Beginning in the late 1920s, she spent 12.5 billion Francs on the Maginot Line that protected her eastern border from Switzerland to the town of Longwy, not far from the strategic city of Sedan, where the Germans had won a great victory over the French in 1870, and where the Allies had won the closing battles of World War I. From there to the sea, France placed the preponderance of her armies. Including those of her allies, these totaled 135 divisions, roughly equal to the 138 that the Germans could bring to the battle. All in all, it was a reasonable strategy for a country that wanted to deter another attack by fixing the weaknesses it had found during the last two.

What about the two sides' weapons? We sometimes assume that the German tanks were so superior that they swept the French from the field. Many people are surprised to learn that one for one, the French tanks were state of the art for the time.[10] Germany, on the other hand, had suffered under a ban on tanks imposed by the allies from 1918 until Hitler's rise to power in 1933. Catching up proved slow, and she did not produce her first fully modern tank until 1939. German armies still had only 349 of this design by May 1940.[11] In addition, France had a great advantage in artillery, which had been the main killer on the battlefield in the last war.

That the Germans would attack surprised no one. Both Britain and France had declared war on Germany on September 3, 1939, two days after the German attack on Poland, and so had eight months to get ready. Likewise, it cannot be said that the German tactics were a surprise. They were a refinement of tactics the Germans had used in their last major offensive in the earlier war and had been studied by both French and British strategists between the wars. As for terrain, the French could read a map and knew about conditions in the Ardennes Forest and the network of narrow roads that traversed it.

The French had even surmised that the Germans might try an attack in that area. To guard against this possibility, the French Second and Ninth Armies took up positions in Sedan and along the Meuse River. Although these formations were staffed with second-rate troops and lacked modern tanks and transport, calculations had shown that the Germans would need nine or ten days to move enough men and artillery through the limited road network in the Ardennes to force a crossing. This would allow French commanders plenty of time to bring up more heavily armed and better trained reinforcements.

To summarize the Allies' position, they knew an attack was coming, and they knew where it was coming—in the 200-mile gap between the Maginot Line and the English Channel. In this area, they had about the same number of troops as their enemy, and this in an era when one was supposed to need a three-to-one advantage in order to mount a successful attack. Most amazing of all, the French had even foreseen the possibility that the Germans would attack where they actually did, and they had prepared an answer for it

With all of this going for them, how could the French and British lose?

What Went Wrong?

Military history will tell you the details of what each unit did on each day of the battle. The important question for strategy, though, is why were the attackers able to make it work? Was it just luck, or was there some underlying principle?

There is one caution. Don't become fascinated by the map. You may be tempted to say to yourself, "It was simple. The allies rushed to the north, and the Germans then cut across the south. I could have won that battle." Could you, now? If the French and British had had the God's-eye view shown in the maps, we would not be studying the battle today. They could have bottled-up the German thrust through the Ardennes since they had the forces available and the plans prepared. An allied loss under what the military call "perfect intelligence" would have been a colossal blunder, not the result of superior German strategy.

Of course, no one was privy to the real map while the battle was raging. This is the key point and one reason why studying the movements of armies has been of such little practical use to business people. What the commanders had, at best, was information about the enemy within a few miles of them. To make things worse, much of this information, as the 19th century military philosopher Carl von Clausewitz observed about information in all wars, was wrong. It was based on misunderstandings, errors in passing data from one person to another, catching a glimpse of trucks and reporting tanks, seeing our tanks and reporting theirs, the effects of fear, panic, and fatigue, and so on.

Anyone who has been in any military operation, even an exercise, knows how much of this there is.

Harvesting the Fruits of Chaos

Such were the conditions that people on both sides had to work with, but somehow the Germans had evolved a way to cope with the chaos. Since they could cope with it, it was in their best interest to create it, and they designed the strategy of the Blitzkrieg to do just that. As for the French, panic and confusion seemed to snowball as the battle progressed.

On the evening of the German attack on Sedan, May 13th, the French 55th Infantry Division began a withdrawal from the west bank of the Meuse River in the face of massive German attacks. As sometimes happens, the retreat got out of control and became a rout. There were incidents, for example, where men far behind the lines abandoned their artillery pieces and began to run to the rear. Writer Len Deighton called it the "greatest tank victory in all the records of warfare," because in truth, the nearest German tanks were still trying to get across the river.[12]

Once one side considers abandoning the field, particularly if it loses the initiative, small setbacks can lead to big disasters, and collapse can occur quickly. This happened with the French. About 36 hours after the Germans crossed the Meuse, for example, the French First Armored Division was moving up to attack the German penetration. It was a powerful force and should have been able to throw a roadblock in front of the fast-moving Germans. As the French force stopped to refuel, however, Major General Erwin Rommel's 7th Panzer Division, joined by the 5th Panzers, ambushed them and destroyed all but 17 out of the original 175 French tanks.[13] Now Rommel did something that characterizes Blitzkrieg warfare. Rather than dig in and "consolidate his position," or otherwise savor the fruits of victory, he proceeded to use his advantage in *time* to neutralize his opponents' forces and weapons. Battle-weary as they must have been, Rommel's troops remounted their vehicles, pressed on to the west, and actually reached the new French defensive line before the French.[14] As one of the German commanders summed it up after the war, "Each minute ahead of the enemy is an advantage."[15]

These two incidents were repeated, on larger and smaller scales, hundreds of times during the campaign. It seemed that fortune chose these two weeks to grant a monopoly to the Germans, and such a "string of luck" is a common indicator that a Boyd-type strategy is working. The chain of fortunate occurrence, however, is an indicator of the strategy, not the strategy itself. Certainly, luck plays a role in war, but it is asking too much to credit luck for something that happened over and over again.

We get a better idea of fundamental causes by looking at what the French commanders were telling each other. Up until the end, they were congratulating themselves on having established new lines to seal off the German attack, as they had done so often during World War I. The situation was improving and the enemy was contained, as they had achieved when they were promising middle grade officers 25 years earlier. The front was, as Churchill promised, being "reestablished."[16]

Even this language gives us a hint about the French predicament. These are terms from the First World War, where in its final year, the Germans had devised tactics similar in many ways to the next war's Blitzkrieg. The allies well remembered, as Churchill's memoirs make clear, that these attacks always ran out of steam, and that the allies were able to establish new front lines and trenches a few miles behind the originals. But this time, the war was fought on different terms.

Look at what British military historian Basil Liddell Hart had to say:

> *The issue turned on the time factor at stage after stage. French counter-movements were repeatedly thrown out of gear because their timing was too slow to catch up with the changing situation . . . The French, trained in the slow-motion methods of World War I, were mentally unfit to cope with the new tempo, and it caused a spreading paralysis among them.*[17]

Or from the British general whom the Germans credit as one of the sources of the Blitzkrieg, J. F. C. Fuller:

It was to employ mobility as a psychological weapon: not to kill but to move; not to move to kill but to move to terrify, to bewilder, to perplex, to cause consternation, doubt and confusion in the rear of the enemy . . . [18]

In other words, the purpose of Blitzkrieg strategy was not so much to cope with chaos, but to cause and then exploit it, and it is this cascading of panic and chaos that accounts for the German's "string of luck."

Incidentally, if you rotate the Blitzkrieg (Map 4) 90 degrees, you get:

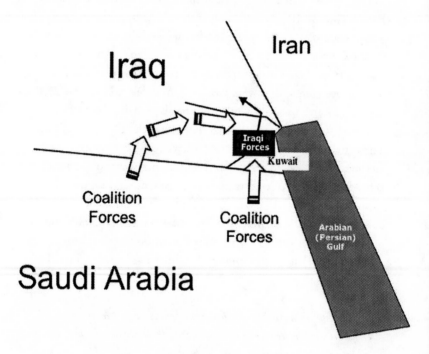

Map 5—Operation DESERT STORM, February 1991

It is too early to reach valid conclusions about the strategy of the Second Gulf War, although it appears to have been Blitzkrieg in nature, but didn't mass and technology win in the First Gulf War?

In these two elements, surprisingly to most Americans, the sides may not have been so far apart. The Iraqi Army had roughly the same number of troops as the Allies, and had the latest Soviet equipment and some excellent artillery. The bulk of the Iraqi force, though, consisted of poorly trained conscript levees, right out of the 19th century, and the "elite" Republican Guard had dug itself into static positions where they were sitting ducks for allied air. So it was in the human elements of training and strategy where the Iraqis came up short—the Allied commander, General Norman Schwarzkopf, remarked later that we could have swapped weapons and the results would have been the same. If there is a fault to the campaign, it was that we occasionally slowed the advance of our most forward forces to permit slower units to catch up. By the end of the war, this delay allowed the Republican Guard and much of its equipment to get up and move back into Iraq, where they suppressed uprisings by the Shi'ite Arabs in the south and the Kurds in the North.

In both the Blitzkrieg and to a lesser extent in Desert Storm, one side was able to use *time* as a device to offset the other's size, technology, position, and even planning. In particular, the winners were able to make things happen that their opponents may have anticipated, but not when their opponents might have expected.

Our view of the world, our "orientation," as Boyd called it, depends heavily on things happening close in time to when we expect them to happen. Mismatches in time—such as when things don't appear to be happening in a continuous and predictable (even if very rapid) manner— can be disorienting. Under stress, disoriented people become demoralized, frustrated, and panicked. Once in this condition, they can easily be defeated, regardless of the weapons that remain in their possession. This is fine for war, but how can such a strategy help businesses?

Blitzkrieg in Business

Boyd created his major work, *Patterns of Conflict*, between about 1975 and 1986 and gave it hundreds of times in briefings to officials in Washington and at military installations around the world. Many of these people later left the military and went into business where they began to use the concept of competing using time as their primary weapon. Time has also been a foundation of business strategy in the Far East, particularly among the Japanese automakers, and researchers were beginning to document this fact at about the same time as Boyd was completing his work.

In 1988, for example, Harvard professor George Stalk published a description of a business campaign that had many of the attributes of the Blitzkrieg including use of time as a most effective weapon.[19] In 1981, Stalk wrote, Yamaha opened an enormous factory and announced that it would become the world's largest motorcycle manufacturer. At that time Honda held the honor and had no intention of relinquishing it.

Most companies in the US as well as in Japan would have challenged force with force and built a factory even larger than Yamaha's. After a while, overcapacity would have reared its ugly head, profits would have turned down, and there would have been the massive layoffs we see in the US auto industry today.

An Alternative to the Obvious

Honda, however, chose to attack through speed and agility. Over the 18 month period of the "H-Y War," Honda introduced 113 new models to replace the 60 it had in the beginning. In contrast, Yamaha was only able to bring out 37.

Honda wasn't cranking out new models for the fun of it. They were learning from how the public accepted, or not, each new model and they made changes accordingly. The result was that both Honda and public tastes evolved during the course of the campaign. By the end of the war, a Yamaha looked drab and unimaginative parked next to a Honda. Yamaha accepted an embarrassing surrender, publicly stating "We want to end the H-Y War. It was our fault."

Why was Honda able to turn up the wick and out-develop Yamaha in new models by 3-to-1? Stalk's analysis is remarkably similar to Liddell Hart's and Fuller's: Honda had "managed structural changes that enabled their operations to execute their processes much faster." Not only were their processes quicker, but Honda knew or learned how to exploit this advantage to achieve a decisive result in the marketplace. Employing a strategy conceptually the same as the Germans' in the Blitzkrieg, Honda used speed, or more accurately, decision cycle time, to create opportunities in the marketplace and then provide products that customers wanted to buy more than they wanted those of the competition. The critical element was that Honda was both learning what these "wants" were and was helping to shape them at the same time.

What's to Come

Don't worry if the mechanics of how the Germans or Honda won are not clear. These details are the subject of the rest of the book. At this point, the only fact of importance is that in two different fields of human competition, war and business, people found ways to use time to offset and eventually render irrelevant their opponent's advantages in such physical parameters as size and technology. The next three chapters lay out Boyd's general concepts for using time in any form of competition and will present specific ideas for employing them in business.

Chapter V describes an organizational climate in which fast decision cycles can flourish. Chapter VI introduces an advanced topic in the theory of time-based competition, the notion of *cheng / ch'i* maneuvers, long recognized by military strategists as fundamental to maneuver warfare and I think you will see that can be equally potent for businesses. Finally, Chapter VII talks a little about applications—tactics, that is. By definition, these are specific to the problem at hand and so beyond the strict scope of a book on strategy. However, Boyd did have something to say on this subject and I trust you will find it useful.

CHAPTER II

Visible Figures Alone

He that would run his company on visible figures alone will soon have neither company nor visible figures to work with. W. Edwards Deming[20]

Is War Relevant to Business?

The highest-level school in the United States Army is the War College at Carlisle Barracks, Pennsylvania. If you pick up any copy of its journal, *Parameters, http://carlisle-www.army.mil/usawc/Parameters/,* and look at the bottom of the front cover, you will see the following words:

"Not To Promote War, But To Preserve Peace."

I also have no intention of glorifying war, but as we saw in the last chapter, there is strategy there. When properly applied, some of the strategies used by the military can overcome huge disadvantages in size and technology, which conventional thinking takes to be decisive. And we see evidence that the same underlying principles can work in business, also overcoming factors that most people think will ensure a competitive advantage.

We need new theories if for no other reason than because conventional ways of thinking gave us Vietnam. In the business world, conventional thinking has consistently failed to produce healthy, competitive enterprises: In automobiles, Chrysler ended its 70-year history and became part of Germany's Daimler-Benz, and GM's market share has fallen by one-third since 1980 despite a $40 billion bill for automation. In computers, proud names such as Wang, Digital Equipment, and Compaq disappeared, and the US airline industry lost $19 billion in 2001 and 2002. These results were not foreordained, since each industry also produced consistently profitable competitors— including Toyota, Dell, and Southwest, respectively.

One of the reasons Boyd's concepts have become so widely accepted, even by people who have never heard of him, is that viewed through his lens, the successes of Toyota, Dell, Southwest, the Germans in 1940, the Israelis in 1956 and 1967, and the Vietnamese in 1975 become readily understandable, even obvious.

Boyd's work represented the culmination of an outburst in strategic thinking that began in the mid-1970s, about the same time as the fall of Saigon. Among the many post-mortem analyses of that conflict, Boyd's followed the logic that since we cannot predict exactly what a future war might look like, we need to find general patterns, the "common elements" as he termed them, that will apply to any battle, conflict, or war. So, rather than engage in a technical "Why did the North Vietnamese win?" inquiry, of which many began at that time, Boyd simply asked: "What does it take to win?" By taking such a general approach, he arrived at ideas that apply to human conflicts in practically whichever arena they occur.

Models of Conflict

What *does* it take to win? This question occupies the rest of the book, which will base its answer on a concept known as *agility*, another word that has lost its original meaning through careless application. Boyd, however, used the term in a specific sense, to mean the ability to rapidly change one's orientation—roughly, worldview—in response to what is happening in the external world. Since Boyd liked the word "agility," and I cannot think of a better one, I will continue to use it and with luck restore its original luster. Agility can be thought of as the output of Boyd's philosophy of maneuver conflict, whereas the cultural attributes, the "principles of the blitzkrieg" that we shall meet in the next chapter, form the input.

Boyd's concept of agility is such a simple idea that traditional military and management strategists often give it little emphasis. Like other simple ideas, however ($E=mc^2$ comes immediately to mind), it has enormous power when applied correctly. The essence of agility and of applying Boyd's ideas to any form of competition is to keep one's orientation well matched to the real world during times of ambiguity, confusion, and rapid change, when the natural tendency is to become disoriented.

In a military conflict, *dis*-orientation can rapidly lead to panic, chaos, and the breakdown of morale and cohesion. When applied to war, Boyd's strategy provides ways to keep one's own orientation intact, while taking active measures to destroy that of the opponent. Time—in particular how long it takes our side to reorient compared to how long it takes the opponent—is Boyd's primary device for accomplishing this, which is why the name "time-based competition" also came to be applied to this approach to strategy.[21]

In business, the effect of agility is perhaps not so obvious. One can, after all, completely discombobulate the competition and then look on as people buy their products and services anyway. It turns out, however—and Stalks's analysis of the Honda-Yamaha War in the previous chapter gives a hint as to why—that agility in Boyd's specific sense is just as powerful a strategy for business.

People can best appreciate Boyd's strategy by contrasting it with other approaches. If you look at a typical book on business strategy, what you will probably find is a discussion of the actions a company can take to try to gain market share or improve profitability. In a sense, it treats business like a giant game of chess, where one side and then the other makes moves and the question of strategy becomes largely a discussion of which moves to use. You will even see terms like "first mover advantage."

The simplest such business strategy is to grow: A competitor makes an acquisition, so we make a larger one. Until the meltdown of the early 21st century, a growth strategy also meant loading up on debt to finance acquisitions. The idea is that once a company achieves sufficient market share, it can dictate the terms of the competition. It can, for example, use economies of scale to drive down prices and eliminate its smaller, less efficient competitors, whereupon it can raise prices and otherwise manipulate the marketplace to produce superior profitability and pay back the costs of the acquisitions. It sounds attractive and it is easy to model the cost savings one can achieve and even the profits one will reap in the end. Players using this strategy included such famous names as SwissAir, Enron, WorldCom, and AOL.

There are many other strategies—you may recall portfolio theory (involving a cast of "stars," "dogs," and "cash cows"), which enjoyed a huge vogue during the 1970s and 1980s, and more recently "core competencies" and "positioning." All of these concepts reflected the idea that strategy involves moves and counter-moves and if played according to the rules of the strategy *du jour*, the result would be improved profitability.

If this were the road to wealth, then the company that was best at applying the correct strategy would make the most money. This statement seems so logical that it may be difficult at first to imagine any alternative. It is easy to see why, once a company starts down this road, it will spend millions of dollars on strategy and strategic planning departments—and the consultants who support them.

Calculating Victory?

If you see strategy as creating better ways to play a "my move—your move" game, then it is inevitable that you will try to foresee what could happen on the various moves. This method has proved successful in analyzing many common games such as chess, where in May 1997, a computer defeated the reigning world champion. It is not unusual in the corporate world to find CEOs using complex graphs and charts to explain to their boards of directors why the acquisition of a competitor— a move in the game—makes good business sense, despite what the competition could do to counter. The calculations underlying their impressive PowerPoint charts are often conceptual brothers of the ones used by the Pentagon to justify the purchase of new weapon systems.

It is *almost* inevitable that you or somebody in your organization will try to formalize the process by collecting data and constructing a computer model. The actual process in business or in war usually includes four steps:

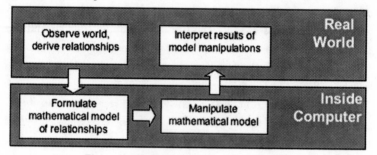

Figure 1—Constructing Computer Models

To illustrate why organizations that follow conventional strategies—and try to map out their implications—are vulnerable to more powerful strategies, let's follow this flow chart and create a simple competitive model. Since war is in the abstract simpler than business, as noted in the previous chapter, it leads to simpler strategic models. For this reason, we'll illustrate conventional strategy by building a model of armed conflict using a standard approach to the subject. Later in this chapter, we'll transition back to how this works in business.

Lanchester's Model

The situation we are going to model consists of two sides, traditionally called "Red" and "Blue." It is also traditional that the side that is supposed to win be Blue and that we be tacitly identified with it. We will assume that each weapon can fire at every weapon on the other side; otherwise we would segment the battlefield until the area we are modeling is small enough so that this is true.

Although this is a simple scenario, it could represent a firefight within some larger battle, and we assume the battle itself to be the cumulative effect of all the firefights within it. For this situation, and thus for the overall battle, what do you think would be the decisive factors in predicting who will win? (You might recall that I defined "conventional thinking" as what most people think will produce victory, in business as in war.) How about the number of weapons each side has and how effective they are? What else could there possibly be? As I promised, at this high level, war is simpler than business, and this is indeed the conventional wisdom of the Pentagon.

So all that's left is to tell the model how many weapons each side has and how good—"effective" in military parlance—they are.

Under the conditions we have described, losses to one side equal the product of the effectiveness of the *other* side's weapons times the number of weapons that the other side has. If you think about it, this is entirely plausible, and it is sort of what "effectiveness" has to mean. For the purposes of this exercise, let's assume that tests have shown that one of our Blue weapons can destroy 1/2 (=.50) of an enemy Red weapon every minute (or equivalently, one enemy weapon every two minutes) on the average. Then in one minute of firing, two of Blue's could destroy one Red weapon, four could destroy two, and so on— the product of effectiveness (.50 in this case) times the number Blue has.[22]

As for the Red weapons let's assume that tests show that they are only half as good (half as "effective") as Blue's, that is, their effectiveness = .25. This means that four Red weapons firing for one minute would destroy, on the average, one Blue weapon. The only step remaining before starting the battle is to tell the model how many weapons each side has. Let's set our Blue force at 100 and to make things fair, since their weapons are only half as effective as Blue's, we'll put in 200 for Red. This is, by the way, the highest level of mathematical sophistication that we will need, although I should point out that in a real Pentagon model, the battle is the result of hundreds of these "engagements" among many different types of weapons, where effectiveness "coefficients" can change during the battle, and so the programs themselves can become quite complex (and expensive.)

The situation at the start of the battle is shown in Figure 2:

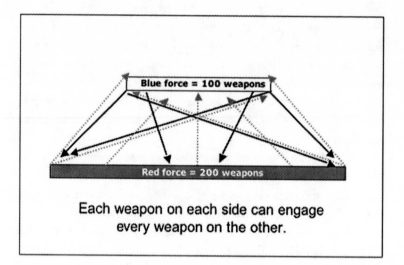

Figure 2—Forces at the Start of the Battle

Thus when the model begins, Red's losses will be:

Red losses = Blue weapons times Blue effectiveness
= 100 times .50
= 50

And:

Blue losses = Red weapons times Red effectiveness
= 200 times .25
= 50

From the way we set up this scenario, things seem evenly matched. Blue has half as many weapons, but they are twice as good, so losses on each side are equal. Real engagements between groups of soldiers usually don't end after one salvo, so let's continue the battle.

Red and Blue each fire another salvo and then another. And then things get very quiet, because if you look at the graph of how many forces each side has left at the start of each salvo, you see that all the Blue forces are dead—or "attritted" as we say in the pristine world of defense modeling:

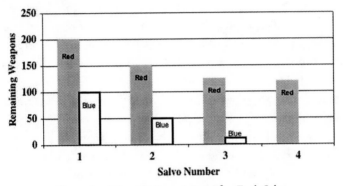

Figure 3—Weapons Remaining After Each Salvo

That is, Blue not only disappears, but does so very quickly, even though its weapons were twice as effective as Red's. If you are a Blue defense strategist, this is not good. So let's suppose that the results of this simulation have reached the highest levels of your government and that you have been assigned the job of figuring out what to do.

Your first thought might be that since it was Red's "numerical superiority" that more than overcame Blue's wonder weapons, Blue should develop cheaper weapons and buy more of them. Although the model predicts that a sufficiently large number of less effective weapons would win, that option is not very appealing in today's world since it would require much larger military forces.[23] Most Western countries rely on volunteer armies nowadays, so recruiting large military forces could prove difficult without resorting to politically unpopular measures such as conscription. Plus it can be much harder to garner political support for low cost weapons in modern democracies since there are fewer subcontracts to distribute among the various political districts.

What is far more common is to try to make up for smaller forces by going the other way, by developing even more advanced technology. In the West, the common interpretation of our model would be to ask, "How good would our weapons have to be to overcome a two-to-one disadvantage in numbers?"

Blue's weapons would have to be better than twice as good—we saw that Blue loses and quickly if its weapons are only twice as good—and in fact they would have to be *four* times more effective just to even the conflict. Since the prospect of an even conflict is not appealing to Blue, they would probably build in some margin of error and launch programs to develop weapons that are perhaps eight or 10 or even 100 times as good. This is not a joke: As the Air force's new wonder weapon, the F-15 fighter, was nearing production in 1973, Air Force generals produced analyses showing that it would be nearly 1,000 times as effective as current Soviet aircraft. One wag suggested that this was great news for the country's budget, since now we would only need to buy 100 of them to defeat the entire Soviet Air Force. The Secretary of Defense approved and Congress voted money for production of the full number (749) anyway, and the generals' briefing was quietly shelved.[24]

To summarize: Once the option of a large, low-cost force is ruled out, the only course open to Blue strategists and politicians is to keep trying for higher and higher levels of high-tech effectiveness. In the real world of defense contracting, this always means higher and higher costs as engineers turn to exotic materials and advanced electronics in their attempts to deliver the desired effectiveness.

Strategy by Machine

Several years ago, an executive with the then-Martin Marietta Corporation, Norm Augustine, figured that such logic would eventually lead to weapons so expensive—although of enormous predicted effectiveness—that the entire defense budget would buy only one. He decided to calculate when this would be. The answer is not in some far dim future, but within the expected lifetimes of many readers: 2054.[25] What this means in concrete terms is that the money actually available for buying military aircraft is funding such small numbers of them, currently 218 in the case of the latest fighter, the F/A-22, that allowing for maintenance, training, and damage from combat, they will be a rare sight over any battlefield.[26]

What we have is a situation where conventional thinking has, with impeccable logic, produced a result that is unacceptable in the real world and that would leave the country less secure if it were followed even partially to its conclusion. We see the same effect in business every day, where companies, for example, use strategic models that tell them to cut costs, and by following the model to its logical conclusion, they reduce the quality of their products and services to the point where they go out of business.[27]

Let's investigate this phenomenon in a little more detail. Going back to the military model, presumably the Blue commander can do simple math, or has a staff that can, and can read the graph as well as the Red commander. So you might be saying to yourself, "This is stupid. Why does the Blue commander just sit there and take it? Nobody would be that dumb." Unfortunately, however, there have been times in history when the loser's orientation seized up and he annihilated himself, exactly as this simple model described.

Let's begin by examining some of these cases to see what type of strategy they represent. One period when many of these battles occurred ran from the mid-1700s up to the end of WW I. This time in history coincided with the great increase in destructiveness (or "effectiveness" as we've been calling it) brought on by modern technology, but it was also a time when strategy appeared trapped in the musket era. Perhaps nothing illustrates this better than the American Civil War.

On July 3, 1863, the third day of the Battle of Gettysburg, Confederate Commander Robert E. Lee ordered Major General George Pickett's fresh division, reinforced by surviving elements of two other divisions, to make one final attack into the center of the Union line. Over the protests of his immediate subordinate, General James Longstreet (who wanted to maneuver around the Federal left flank), the attack was made. One cannot fault the valor or determination of the men who made it: As a result of his eponymous "charge," Pickett lost about 75% of the men in his division, while failing to take the federal lines.[28] Although we honor the participants for their dedication and their bravery, such loss of life for no gain brings no glory to those who ordered it. It should also lead citizens to wonder if they have the right people leading their armies.

Another particularly famous incident of this sort occurred during the Crimean War (between Britain and Russia) in 1854. At one point in the Battle of Balaklava, the 600 cavalrymen of the British Light Brigade charged the massed guns of the Russians. Despite horrendous losses, the British continued their attack. Only 150 of them made it back to their own lines, leading a French observer to note wryly, "*C'est magnifique, ma c'est ne pas la guerre.*"[29] British Poet Laureate at the time, Alfred Lord Tennyson, was less amused: "Someone had blundered."

The message is not that these examples prove that the Lanchester strategy is right or wrong. What it does show is that many people have followed the strategic logic crudely simulated by the Lanchester model to the bitter end. They have "validated" the model by leaving piles of bodies on the battlefield. Anytime a military commander gets into a "battle of attrition," as these Lanchester engagements are called, and gets his people ground into the dust, he deserves the "blunder" label, even if he wins.

Instead of something useful, conventional thinking produced strategies that led to some of the worst disasters in military history. Of course, one could ask the same question about business strategies and leaders who run their organizations into the ground, disrupting the lives of thousands of people in their companies who were depending on their senior management to employ successful strategies.

W. Edwards Deming, a quote from whom opened this chapter, recommended looking at the world in terms of "special" and "common" causes. If in your organization you have a small number of people making mistakes and performing poorly, it's probably their fault. You should spend your time working with them, or transfer them to other jobs, or if neither of those options is feasible, remove them. If it's much more than 10%, though, then it's the system's fault and you should put your effort into fixing the system and quit blaming or exhorting the people in it.

As we have seen, poor strategy was so widespread that there must have been something wrong with the entire system of warfare, that is, how it was generally studied and taught—conventional thinking, in other words.

The Blitzkrieg Wasn't a Fluke

After all, Hooker planned very well, and although he executed poorly his advantage in numbers was large enough to rub out a great many mistakes. Bruce Catton on Union General Joseph Hooker who lost to a much smaller force led by Lee at Chancellorsville, May 1863.[30]

There is a saying that the battle is not always to the strong, but that's the way to bet. If by stronger, you mean bigger, or more advanced technologically, you are going to lose your bet fairly often even if you're wagering (or investing in) business. Wal-Mart, which did not even exist when the list was started, sits atop the Fortune 500, while erstwhile retailing titans suffer: As this is written, Sears is number 32, JCPenney is 50th, K-Mart is in bankruptcy, and Montgomery Ward is gone. There have always been strategists down through history, in the East in particular, who have held the "bigger is better" notion in special contempt. The noted Chinese strategist Sun Tzu (c. 5th century B.C.), who is still widely studied today, dismissed the fascination with size thusly: "Numbers alone confer no advantage."[31] Japan's favorite strategist, the 17th Century samurai warrior-philosopher, Miyamoto Musashi, wrote with blunt contempt that "it does not matter who is stronger or who is faster."[32]

In the next chapter, we will explore ways smaller forces can defeat larger opponents. For now, you can see the truth of Sun Tzu's remark by looking at how often the smaller side has actually won, even in the West:

Quite Often the Smaller, or Less Technologically Advanced Side Wins

Arabs vs. Persia, Byzantine Empire, etc.	633-732
Mongols vs. China, Russia, Moslems, etc.	1211-1260
American Colonies vs. Great Britain	1775-1781

Germany vs. France & England	1940
Israel vs. Arab States	1948-1973
Algeria vs. France	1954-1961
Vietnam vs. United States	1958-1975
Afghanistan vs. USSR	1980-1989
Chad vs. Libya	1987
Chechnya vs. Russia	1991-1996

Winner in **bold**.

How often does the smaller side win? Certainly not all the time, and the historical evidence suggests that numbers do play a role. A recent study of 625 battles from 1600 to 1973, for example, concluded that having a larger force does indeed improve the chances of victory but not by enough to overcome other factors, which they identified as "leadership skills" and "troop morale."[33] This is the "everything else being equal, size matters" argument. Why in the world, you should ask yourself, would one go into battle with "everything else being equal," especially concerning the factors known to produce victory? The whole purpose of strategy is to stack these as heavily as possible in our favor.

Could culture or some particular national trait be responsible for military brilliance? It seems unlikely since a winner in one period can seem to forget everything it learned almost overnight. Two months after his brilliant maneuvering victory at Chancellorsville, for example, Lee ordered Pickett to attack the Union center at Gettysburg and in the process destroyed the myth that farmers from the South would always defeat city boys from the North.

It can happen to entire countries. By 1969, North Vietnam had worn down US political will, causing our withdrawal and leading to their conquest of the South in 1975. Three years later Vietnam became bogged down in a quagmire of its own in Cambodia with ultimately the same result—withdrawal. The Soviet Union gloated over the US debacle in Vietnam, then marched into Afghanistan. Tiny Israel took on the entire Arab world between 1948 and 1973 and won. Yet the Israelis were forced to retreat from their 1982 preemptive war against Lebanon, and their mighty army has yet to deal with civilian uprisings—the Palestinian *intifadas*—or provide much security against suicide bombers. So whatever is producing these counter-intuitive results does not seem to be the special property of any particular country or society.

What all of this suggests is that individual brilliance alone cannot account for strategies where smaller, less technologically advanced forces win, since, following Deming, such effects should only account for something less than 10% of battles. The study cited above suggested that the true number is over 25%, more than can be ascribed to numbers or technology alone. There must be something else there, some other way of looking at strategy that can enable smaller "weaker" forces to win far more often than conventional thinking would suggest.

Does the same apply to business? One need only compare Toyota to General Motors in 1946 or Wal-Mart to Sears in 1962 with where they are today.

There's Something Going On Here

The human heart, and the psychology of the individual fighting man, have always been the ruling factors in warfare, transcending the importance of numbers and equipment. This old maxim held during World War II and I think it will always do so.[34] Major General F. W. von Mellenthin (1956)

In May 1863, at about the time Lee was befuddling Hooker at Chancellorsville, Confederate cavalryman Nathan Bedford Forrest was chasing a regiment of Union cavalry across a wide swath of northern Alabama, finally cornering them a few miles west of the Georgia border near the town of Cedar Bluff. Forrest demanded surrender, and the Union commander, a colonel named Abel D. Streight, refused. At that point, one of Forrest's men rode up and asked for orders for his regiment, which was coming in from the north, followed shortly by another requesting orders for a regiment approaching from the south. Streight, who could also hear sounds of large amounts of equipment moving in the distance, figured the game was over and honorably surrendered his 1700 men to what turned out (to his horror) to be Forrest's 350, less than one-quarter of one fully manned regiment. He was still demanding his guns back when Forrest put his arm around him and uttered those immortal words of strategy, "Ah Colonel, all is fair in love and war, you know."[35]

If you dig a little, you can find that throughout history, there has been an undercurrent of strategists who looked at war in this light, and not as some type of collection of pieces on a game board. For example:

- "All warfare is based upon deception."—Sun Tzu
- "War is trickery."—Muhammad, Prophet of Islam
- "Mystify, mislead and surprise"—Stonewall Jackson
- "I put the scare on them, and I keep it on."—Nathan Bedford Forrest

Notice that not one held that you win by multiplying weapon effectiveness times the square of the number of weapons (or some such). In fact, the things that these observers found important are impossible to capture in a computer program, since it is difficult to get silicon to panic.[36]

If you keep exploring, you can find a few strategists, even in the West, who came to similar conclusions. A former commander of all US Army troops in Europe, and holder of a distinguished war record himself, summed this all up with, "We have been led astray by computerized war games and map exercises because the primary determinant of victory in these exercises is a preponderance of firepower . . ."[37] The models could only capture what could be quantified, and had to gloss over such critical factors as generalship, training, surprise, and fatigue. Other "soft" but decisive effects, which conventional thinking finds difficult but strategists insist on, include:

Things We Want To Have On Our Side:

- Sense of Mission
- Morale
- Leadership
- Harmony
- Teamwork

Which Allow Us To:

- Appear Ambiguous
- Be Deceptive
- Generate Surprise & Panic
- Seize & Keep The Initiative
- Create & Exploit Opportunities

Which Cause These In The Enemy:

- Bickering
- Scapegoating
- Confusion
- Panic
- Rout
- Mass Defections & Surrender

Table I—What Wins

Where Boyd made his great contribution was not in drawing up this list, for its elements can all be found in the earliest works on strategy, but by showing that they still apply in this era of $200 million fighter aircraft and by giving some concrete advice on how to generate and employ them.

Modeling in Business

I certainly have no objection to model building, since I have spent the majority of my professional career in that occupation. There are many situations that call for models and other "hard" analytical techniques. Where the solution to our problem depends on underlying physical processes, as in an engineering simulation, we can extract relationships and build models that make useful predictions and which may provide answers that we can get no other way. But this type of situation—"man against nature"—does not concern strategy. Here we enter the arena of "thinking human against thinking human," and so if a model, or any step-by-step method, is to guide strategy, it must capture those things that are important in winning against a hostile intelligence, which we must assume is as good at running mathematical models as we are.

We have seen in the preceding sections that military models deal in the "hard" factors that can be quantified, things like the sizes of the opposing forces and the levels of technological sophistication of their weapons. We have also seen that except for battles of attrition and military blunders, neither of these has played a dominant role in deciding the outcome of battles down through history.

Could the same be true of business?

Macroeconomic and Business Models

Some readers may have noticed a parallel between using models and analytical techniques as the bases of strategy, and the debate over using similar methods as the foundation of economic policy. Essentially, these programs consist of thousands of equations that are supposed to describe the relationships between various components of the economy. So there might be a set of equations that tie the inflation rate to stock prices, and another set that relates unemployment to housing starts, and so on. The idea is that once all these equations are joined together, you can raise the discount by one-half point, and the model will tell you the effect on unemployment (or whatever).

Unlike military models, where we hope we never get the opportunity to check our creations against the real world, we can test econometric models every day. Simply watch what the Fed does to the discount rate and see what happens to unemployment. So you might think that by now, someone would have invented a model of the economy that works. Then, at least in theory, economic policymaking would be simple: Play with the model until you get a result you like (or can live with) and then implement the policy (the model inputs) that produced it.

Why, then, are we greeted evening after evening by congressional debates on whether something as simple as eliminating taxes on corporate dividends would be good for the economy? Will it increase the deficit or stimulate investment? It all depends on whether you like the models run for the *Wall Street Journal* or those paid for by *The New York Times*.

Why should this be the state of affairs? People have spent a lot of money on these models, and the best are all based, to the extent possible, on relationships we actually observe in the real world. Perhaps the problem is, as I have suggested for strategy, that modeling by its very nature cannot address the underlying basis of economics.

Nobel Laureate Frederick Hayek eloquently makes this case in his book, *The Fatal Conceit*. Hayek inveighed against the notion of ever being able to plan a productive economy. He argues that formal planning methodologies—which are models of how an economy works—do not capture what really drives a competitive economy, in particular the information processed through decisions made daily by millions of buyers and sellers. Conversely, countries that try to run their economies through a central state planning mechanism cannot process information nearly as well as the multitude of players in a decentralized system. Hayek's theories were validated in the last half of the 20th century, when countries that relied on Soviet-style planning collapsed in competition with those that evolved decentralized, capitalist economies.

Another reason economies are impossible to model involves the messy presence of human beings. Financially massive organizations warp the environment they inhabit much like the way gravitationally massive bodies warp space-time in physics: Normal rules do not apply to them. Giant companies influence Congress, the executive branch, and local governing bodies to pass legislation they want—granting them subsidies, protection, environmental relief, favorable tax status, and so on—and otherwise treat them in ways that are perfectly legal, but outside what the equations of economics predict.[38]

These favors can range from protective tariffs to outright grants (often inserted by pet Congressional representatives into obscure sections of appropriation bills) to programs that continue to bleed tax dollars long after any need for them has disappeared. As an aside, this last effect—often called "pork"—is well known to those in defense, and former President Eisenhower warned of it in his Farewell Address (January 1961):

> *In the councils of government, we must guard against the acquisition of unwarranted influence, whether sought or unsought, by the military-industrial complex. The potential for the disastrous rise of misplaced power exists and will persist.*

These are the soft, political, impossible-to-model but critical aspects of the economy. Any company that attempted to ignore them, to predict in a step-by-step fashion the results of its moves, creates a form of macroeconomic model because it is also predicting effects on at least part of the larger economy. So it will fall victim to the limitations of any such model—including Hayek's information processing arguments and political activities that change the rules. The upshot will be a strategy that works no better for business than did its counterparts for war: A company using such a model would make itself vulnerable to competitors who better understand the real economy.

Strategy itself begins where hard, provable techniques leave off. There must be something more, and what this something more might be is the subject of the rest of this book.

CHAPTER III

Sting Like a Bee

We think perhaps we may have gotten inside of the enemy's decision-making cycle and arrived with a tempo that put us in place before they could respond to the impending threat that now is a matter of history. US Army Brigadier General Vincent Brooks, Doha, Qatar, April 4, 2003[39]

Why Some Sides Always Seem to Win

In the last chapter, I defined "effectiveness" solely in terms of numbers and types of equipment. The idea was to illustrate conventional thinking in the military sector. It can be argued that by using this definition, I have deliberately created a strawman that is easy to demolish. It may be easy to demolish, intellectually, but it does represent how the military-industrial complex views the essence of war. *The Wall Street Journal,* for example, recently carried a story called "Wars of the Future."[40] In it, the *Journal* describes the additional billions of dollars the Pentagon's new budget devotes to missile defense, high-speed communications equipment, a new aircraft carrier, and conversion of cold-war era ballistic missile submarines. It concludes with a lament that the new wonder weapons may not be ready until after George W. Bush's second term (which would end in January 2009) "But without them the U.S. won't be prepared to fight and win the wars of the future."

This article is typical, and not only of pro-business publications like the *Journal*. Frankly, it is difficult to see how this exotic hardware would have prevented—or can prevent in the future—attacks like those of September 11, 2001, which cost al-Qa'ida perhaps $200,000 and required no weapons development program.[41] What al-Qa'ida did use were the factors that have produced victory in combat, such as those in the list in Table I, chapter II. Since the style of warfare favored by terrorists and their kin in revolutionary groups, narcotrafficking organizations, and just plain criminal syndicates seems to represent the real future of conflict—and there is even a thriving subset of the business publishing genre for books starting with "Guerilla"—let's explore these factors further.

Boyd was famous for browbeating his audiences with the mantra, "People, ideas, and hardware—*in that order!*" What we have seen so far reinforces Boyd's conclusion. In all the battles and business examples noted in chapter II, as well as in the Pentagon and World Trade Center attacks, groups of dedicated people found and exploited weaknesses in their larger and better-financed adversaries.

The question is, was it luck, or is there some underlying pattern that allows this to happen? In the last chapter, we saw that to create an explicit model of combat, business, or the economy, we had to assume that these activities proceeded according to predictable, mathematical patterns—that they form *systems*.[42] We also found that on many occasions, the smaller or less technologically advanced side won, confounding the predictions of the models.

The reason for this reversal, in business and in war, appears to be that these smaller organizations were able to avoid or negate the larger's advantages in size and strength. Somehow they had managed *not* to become systems in the eyes of their larger opponents. *This might lead one to suspect that in any competitive endeavor, if you can be modeled ("sand-tabled," as Boyd referred to it) you aren't using strategy at all, and you can be defeated.*

Otherwise the smaller side might occasionally have won by luck, but most likely there would be no Toyota, which was much smaller than GM at the end of World War II, no Dell, no Wal-Mart, no Microsoft, and no Southwest Airlines. These companies have all survived and prospered long enough that we can safely rule out luck as the main reason for their success.

How does the smaller side get away with it and win? He doesn't always, of course. The Confederacy lost to the Union, Poland lost to Germany, Finland to Russia, and Germany to practically the rest of the world. The research cited in the last chapter indicated that by picking the larger or more technologically advanced side, you can predict victory in just less than 75% of the battles studied. This sounds impressive, until you recall that by flipping a coin, you can predict victory 50% of the time. The fact that the smaller side does win, and not infrequently, is what excites our interest. To start to answer the question of what it takes to win—what it takes to put Boyd's trinity to useful effect—let's continue with our initial case study, the Blitzkrieg.

Key Attributes of the Blitzkrieg

Armies that engage in Blitzkrieg and maneuver warfare in general differ in fundamental ways from armies designed to conduct attrition warfare. Blitzkrieg strategies do not aim to execute the same maneuvers as other forms of warfare, such as charging across no man's land, only more quickly.[43] In a typical operation, blitzing units don't expose themselves to direct enemy fire any more than absolutely necessary. They seem to loom up from out of nowhere to overwhelm a section of the enemy's line, then penetrate to create surprise and confusion in the rear. It is this abrupt, unexpected, and disorienting pattern of action that forms the basis of his strategy.[44]

The people who created this style of warfare in the late 19th and first part of the 20th centuries realized early on that it required a type of discipline different from the mindless obedience to orders that characterized the Prussian armies of Frederick the Great in the mid-1700s. Modern weapons are extremely lethal and opportunities to surprise and shock an intelligent enemy are fleeting. Soldiers at all levels must be free to—must be required to—use their creativity, intelligence, and initiatives to work around the enemy's weapons and generate and exploit opportunities.

Gradually the Prussians and others largely within Germany evolved a culture that fostered this type of fighting spirit. Although its elements can all be found in Sun Tzu, the Germans were the first to codify it in its present form and to give it the terminology we use today. It conveys "fighting power," to use the title of a book by Martin van Creveld, who insisted that the German army of WWII possessed more of it than any other modern military force.[45] This is high praise from the dean of Israeli defense analysts.

The rest of this chapter uses the climate of the Blitzkrieg to illustrate several principles of strategy. Some people may object, citing the terrible crimes committed by the Nazis against whoever did not fit their mold of acceptability. By using German strategy, and their own words to describe it, are we not condoning or even glorifying Nazi actions?

This is not my intention. One could argue that given the limitations of their system—the Nazis' absolute refusal to learn anything from their Jewish population, who included many of Germany's most highly educated citizens, for example—they had put themselves at an enormous disadvantage relative to the rest of the world. I believe this is correct, and that they nearly won anyway gives further evidence to how good their strategy was. Those who would oppose fascist and totalitarian movements in the future would do well to consider this.

Another reason for studying the Blitzkrieg is that it was the case most intensely examined by the American defense strategists who derived the concepts in this book. They were struck by the brevity of the campaign and low number of casualties, both of these in contrast to the years-long bloodbaths which had been fought over this same terrain a mere quarter century before.

A final reason why strategists focused on the Blitzkrieg was that many of the people on both sides were still alive and willing to talk in detail about their experiences. This allowed the type of give and take needed to develop a coherent theory of what happened. In fact, other armies, notably the Israelis, use these principles today, and a study of guerilla warfare—or "fourth generation warfare," as it is becoming known—reveals the same characteristics.[46] Few of these, however, were willing to sit down and go into detail on strategies, which, particularly in the cases of the Israelis and operatives from al-Qa'ida, they were still employing.

Thus, the Blitzkrieg provided an almost ideal case study for the strategist, despite its connections to an abhorrent cause. By noting what American researchers saw in the German strategy, and why it worked, we can begin to derive ideas that will prove useful in other competitive endeavors, namely business.

After the war, American strategists did get the opportunity to talk at length with many of the practitioners of the Blitzkrieg. Amidst all the war stories, a pattern became clear: The roots of success in 1940 lay in the German system for dealing with people; it was cultural, rather than technical. Here, I am using "cultural" in the sense of "business culture," not as a national trait. From his conversations with the German generals and his study of their experiences and doctrine, Boyd extracted the four concepts shown below as the primary reasons for the Germans' success: You don't have to be a tank commander in central Europe to exploit these cultural properties. Boyd called them "an organizational climate for operational success," and the organization can be a business, a political campaign, or, of course, an army.

Key Attributes of the Blitzkrieg

- *Einheit:* Mutual trust, unity, and cohesion
- *Fingerspitzengefühl:* Intuitive feel, especially for complex and potentially chaotic situations
- *Auftragstaktik:* Mission, generally considered as a contract between superior and subordinate
- *Schwerpunkt:* Any concept that provides focus and direction to the operation

This climate will give a competitive advantage to any group of people who must work together in a confusing and threatening environment. Chapter V will discuss in detail how these principles apply to business, so for now, let's take a brief first look at the various components.

For the same reason that students of lean production continue to use the original Japanese terms, such as *kanban, kaizen,* and *jidoka,* I will from time to time throw in these German words. The purpose is to remind readers that translations are imprecise and possibly misleading. There are no English words that capture the complete meanings and connotations of these words.

Einheit: *Mutual Trust*

Mutual trust, unity, and cohesion underlie everything. The military drives this point home to their young combat leaders, who face perhaps the most difficult "management" challenge there is. Pick up any good book on military leadership—I particularly like *Small Unit Leadership: A Commonsense Approach*[47] by retired US Army Colonel Mike Malone because of the practical advice this decorated combat infantry leader gives young officers and NCOs. You cannot, he admonishes, give in to the urge to check and control everybody. In the heat of battle, there isn't time. You have to trust your soldiers and subordinate leaders to do the right thing under the stress of combat. But, and this is the key point, this trust cannot be wished for or assumed. It must be earned through training and working together, as the German Army did between the two world wars when it was reduced to a small core of career professionals (an "unintended consequence" of the surrender terms imposed by the Allies at Versailles.)

The original German word, by the way, has a root meaning "one," and the word has a connotation of a unit (of measurement or of an organization), or even a device.

It is no accident that this formulation of "mutual trust" heads the Blitzkrieg list. One of the contributors to the Blitzkrieg concept was, oddly enough, a British strategist, J. F. C. Fuller, whose works before WW II were carefully studied by the Germans. Although General Fuller was a pioneer of modern mechanized warfare, he also wrote that " . . . the essential factor in primitive tribal warfare was concord between members of the tribe . . . Normally the same holds true among civilized states."[48]

Bill Lind, a colleague of Boyd's and the author of one of the classics of maneuver warfare, a book that belongs on every strategist's bookshelf, *Maneuver Warfare Handbook*,[49] wrote that:

> *Both leadership and monitoring are valueless without trust. The "contracts"... of intent and mission express that trust ... that his subordinates will understand and carry out his desires and trust by his subordinates that they will be supported when exercising their initiative.*

If there is a universally accepted truth in military science, the fundamental role played by cohesion, unity, and trust may be it. Twenty-four hundred years before Fuller, Sun Tzu had concluded that, "He whose ranks are united in purpose will be victorious."[50] The Arab historian ibn Khaldun, who is generally credited with writing the first modern analysis of history, echoed this theme in 1377 A.D., "What is in fact proven to make for superiority is the situation with regard to group feeling." The rule is simple: The side with the stronger group feeling has a great advantage.[51]

Thus German General Heinz Gaedcke, when asked about what makes a good commander, replied that first, they did not lead from the rear, and second, "they commanded on the basis of mutual trust."[52] Postwar military analysts agreed: "Teamwork was the key to German superiority."[53]

During its period of greatest triumph, from 1948 to 1973, the Israeli Army went to great lengths to build mutual trust. You could not, for example, come into the army as an officer. Everybody started as an 18-year old draftee or volunteer. From among this crowd, the best were selected to become NCOs and finally officers. Now here is the critical idea: While they were moving up, from squad leader to platoon leader and company commander, they generally stayed in their original units. All of the officers and sergeants shared a common background, knew each other's strengths and weaknesses, and could communicate rapidly and accurately using very few words.

So perhaps it is ironic that today, some Israelis credit trust for whatever success was achieved by the first *intifada*, the largely unarmed Palestinian uprising that caused Israel far more problems than the Arab armies ever did. *Intifada* leaders, it turns out, built mutual trust through years of organizing within Israeli prison camps. This trust on a person-to-person level had proven stronger than the factional rivalries that divided these leaders before they were jailed.

The leadership of the *intifada* earned mutual trust through their shared experiences in prison. Israeli military leaders acquired it through a similar crucible, by working and fighting alongside each other during the constant crises and frequent wars of the country's early history. Such an anvil of shared experience appears to be a necessary ingredient in forging a bond of trust.

Boyd concluded that to be most effective, training and shared experiences must expose the organization to more and more complex and dangerous situations so that people finally learn to trust each other in the confusion of conflict. The result can win wars:

> *"Through the long years of fighting in hard conditions of dangers and privations, our officers and men have loved each other like blood brothers, sharing hardships and joys together, united for life and in death."*
> North Vietnamese Defense Minister Vo Nguyen Giap (1961—
> before significant numbers of US forces had entered the conflict)[54]

Certainly this is propaganda, and probably published for our benefit. That's the point: This is what Giap thought would impress his foreign readers. He didn't have the technology or the size to go head-to-head with the United States, but his message was that he wasn't going to fold easily, either. And of course, he didn't.

Fingerspitzengefühl: *Intuitive Skill*

Literally a fingertip feeling or sensation, it is usually translated as "intuitive skill or knowledge." It provides its owner an uncanny insight into confusing and chaotic situations and is often described as the "ability to feel the battle." During the North African campaign, the British ascribed this seemingly mystical quality to Rommel because he always seemed to know what the British were going to do. Time and again, the Desert Fox would appear out of nowhere to scatter British units and sow terror and destruction.

As Gaedcke described it, at the right moment, "for which they all had a sure feel, (his commanders) would step into their airplanes or vehicles and go to the critical point of action to see whether everything was in order—or, occasionally, to really shake things up."[55]

General F. W. von Mellenthin, who as a junior officer participated in the attack on France, noted that the German units crossing the Meuse on May 14, 1940, had "practiced and rehearsed their roles for months." Their French opponents were not so well prepared:

> *Fortunately, the French found it difficult to improvise (a counterattack) at short notice; their tanks moved slowly and clumsily and by the time they got into action, our antitank guns were arriving . . . although the French attacked courageously, they showed little skill, and soon nearly 50 of their tanks were burning on the battlefield.[56]*

Zen and other oriental philosophies talk at great length about intuitive knowledge, but they also stress that it comes through years of experience and self-discipline. In medieval Japan, samurai warriors practiced with the long sword until it became as an extension of their arm. When the fight starts, you don't have time to stop and think about the fundamentals. In fact, one of the goals of Japanese samurai strategy was to cause this very "stopping" of the mind in their opponents.

Auftrag: *The Contract of Leadership*

Once your team has achieved a high level of competence in performing individual and unit tasks, and where most communication is implicit and the need for written instructions is relatively rare, then you can start leading through missions—as opposed to by assigning tasks, for example. Although hierarchies are not the only type of human organization, I am going to use terms like "subordinate" *faute de mieux.* If this bothers you, substitute "the person who has the vision for what needs to be done" for "superior" and "a person whom he or she is going to ask to help accomplish it" for "subordinate." It should be noted, though, that there are few examples of effective combat units that were participatory democracies.

The German word *Auftrag*, by the way, involves notions like assignment, mission, commission, mandate, order (as in "purchase order"), bid, and even request. The connotation in the military sense was more "contract," implying some degree of negotiation and mutual agreement than simply a top down task or order. Following Boyd, I am going to use the noun *Auftrag*, in place of the more common (and longer) *Auftragstaktik*, since the English word "tactic" can convey a misleading impression of this concept.

Lind placed maneuver-type orders near the top of his list of elements in maneuver warfare:

> *A maneuver warfare military believes it is better to have high levels of initiative among subordinate officers, with a resultant rapid Boyd Cycle, even if the price is some mistakes.*

In strategy, the mission concept was designed to allow maximum room for individual initiative, while still accomplishing the unit's mission during the chaos of war. A mission order can be thought of as a virtual contract between superior and subordinate. If I am your superior, and I order you to disrupt and delay enemy forces east of XYZ River, you have two choices. You can accept, in which case enemy forces east of XYZ River are disrupted and delayed. There is no excuse for anything else, even if you and all your people get killed trying. Note that how you accomplish the mission is up to you, within any constraints that I put into the order.

Your other choice, if you believe that you do not have the resources to carry out the order, or that it is just plain dumb, is to challenge it. The German system encouraged this, but once agreement was reached, the superior could assume that the mission would be accomplished.

Now this sounds brutal, a caricature of Prussian discipline. Such a contract, though, is effective only as part of an overall cultural milieu that includes such other elements as mutual trust and an intuitive sense of strategy. If we have built sufficient trust based on mutual experience, I know what you are capable of, and I trust you to do it if you agree to it. You trust me not to order you to do something that you cannot do or that will endanger you for no important strategic reason. How do we all know these things? Because we have trained and fought together over an extended time and earned this level of trust. We can make these decisions rapidly and accurately because of our intuitive competence.

Schwerpunkt: *Focus and Direction*

This brings us to *Schwerpunkt*, which is any device or concept that gives focus and direction to our efforts. The word literally translates as "hard/difficult point," but its real meaning is more like center of gravity, focal point, or main focus. It can also mean "emphasis."

The distinguishing characteristic of an effective focus is that all other activities of the organization must support it and that the people conducting these activities understand what the main effort is and know that they must support it. Conversely, subordinates are expected to use their own initiatives to exploit opportunities, even if it means setting aside a previously issued order, whenever they can further the accomplishment of the focusing-and-directing mission (communicating this change back to the commander, of course). As you can see, this is a powerful concept for motivating subordinates, while at the same time harmonizing their energy to accomplish the commander's intent.[57]

For the attack on France, the panzer thrust in the southern sector of the campaign provided focus and direction for the whole operation. All the activity at the north was intended to set up the allies, mentally and physically, for the armored penetration in the south. Similarly in the First Gulf War (Desert Storm), the Marines offshore, and a visible massing of forces next to Kuwait, set up Saddam Hussein for Schwarzkopf's famous left hook (Map 5 in chapter I.) This notion of "setting-up" activities followed by a knockout punch is as old a concept as mutual trust. Its known roots go back thousands of years, and the ancient Chinese even had expressions for this type of strategy, calling the setting-up, "*cheng* maneuvers," to be followed at the decisive moment by the "*ch'i*" knockout punch.[58] Chapter VI will explore the *cheng/ch'i* pattern further and illustrate how it can be applied in business.

By the middle of the 17th century in Japan the concept of focus had evolved to a high level of sophistication and had taken on the psychological overtones that we will examine later in this chapter. In his classic on strategy, *A Book of Five Rings* (1645), the samurai who is best known in the West, Miyamoto Musashi, removed the concept from the physical world entirely by designating the spirit of the opponent as the focus: Do not even consider risking a decision by cold steel until you have defeated the enemy's will to fight.[59]

This is a revealing statement by a man reported to have won some sixty bouts, virtually all of which ended in the death of his opponent (not surprising, when you consider that the samurai long sword, the *tachi*, was a four foot blade of steel, sharp as a modern razor, and strong enough to chop cleanly through a water pipe.) Once you accept Musashi's dictum as a strategic principle, then you might ask how to carry it out, how to actually defeat the opponent's spirit. Musashi was no mystic, and he grounded all his methods in real actions his students could take. We will encounter him and his techniques many times in this book.

The ability to rapidly shift the focus of one's efforts is a key element in how a smaller force defeats a larger, since it enables the smaller force to create and exploit opportunities before the larger force can marshal reinforcements. Lind notes, and this is especially relevant to business, that the focus is often a concept rather than a unit, and so shifting it requires a mental as well as a physical change. Chapter V will explore this notion further.

So you won't think that I am glorifying everything the German Army did, it is interesting to note that the Germans themselves violated the focus-and-direction principle one year after their Blitzkrieg had so spectacularly defeated France. In his critique of the attack on Russia, Field Marshal Gerd von Runstedt, commander of Army Group A, which spearheaded the Blitzkrieg (Map 4), noted that instead of a clearly designated *Schwerpunkt* against Leningrad in the north, Moscow in the center, or Stalingrad in the south, they simply tried all three[60]. Part of the reason for this strategic lapse undoubtedly came from the dismal performance of Soviet troops against Finland in the Russo-Finnish War (1939-1940, and another example of a small force dealing defeat after defeat upon a larger one until numbers finally wore them down), and part reflected Hitler's belief in the innate superiority of some "Aryan race." In any case, an arrogant disrespect for the opponent has proven fatal in most every arena of competition.

Implicit Communication

The German organizational climate encouraged people to act, and to take the initiative, even during the terror and chaos of war. Within this climate, the principles of mutual trust and intuitive competence make much of implicit communication, as opposed to detailed, written instructions. The Germans felt they had no alternative. As the Chief of the Prussian General Staff in the Franco-Prussian War (1870-71), Field Marshal Helmuth von Moltke, observed in the mid-1800s, the greater risk is the loss of time that comes from always trying to be explicit.[61] Or as General Gaedcke commented about his unit in WW II, if he had tried to write everything down, "we would have been too late with every attack we ever attempted."[62]

The notion of implicit communication also has deep roots in Zen, another of Boyd's primary influences. Thomas Cleary, in his *The Japanese Art of War* (which may have been Boyd's all time favorite book, next to Sun Tzu itself) emphasizes the importance Zen places on mind-to-mind communication. As Cleary notes, this has nothing to do with telepathy or other mystical nonsense but clearly means the transmission of Zen through objective experience, that is, through actions in the real world, which is how Boyd and the maneuver warfare theorists build mutual trust and unit cohesion.[63]

It is true that the Germans did not always apply these principles well, and sometimes forgot them entirely. Len Deighton even claims that there was only one true Blitzkrieg, the May 1940 attack on France.[64] Defense analyst and Boyd acolyte Pierre M. Sprey,[65] who translated and assisted in several of Boyd's interviews with the German generals, estimated that the climate was only fully implemented by maybe one-half of one percent of the army—the small circle around Heinz Guderian that Sprey calls "brilliant rebels." In this sense, the Israeli Army of 1956 and 1967 was superior, man for man, to the German Army of 1940.[66]

Meanwhile, Back in The States

In the early 1950s, then-Lieutenant John Boyd noticed, as did many others, that although the best Russian fighter of the Korean War, the MiG-15, was roughly equal to his F-86 (and in some ways was even better), Americans won ten air battles for every one they lost. Sure, part of this was better training, but even when we got our hands on MiGs later on, and flew them with our own pilots, the F-86 still won more than it should.

Many years later, Boyd tried using his "energy maneuverability" concept to explain why the F-86 was able to compile such a lopsided record. Energy maneuverability (EM) is a mathematical technique for telling under what conditions one fighter will be able to turn tighter or accelerate faster than another. Since experience had shown that the fighter that could turn or accelerate better usually gained a decisive advantage, EM had become the official fighter doctrine of the Air Force. Even EM, though, could not explain the F-86's advantage because the MiG's numbers were at least as good at many altitude and airspeed combinations and at some altitudes and at certain airspeeds, better. The secret turned out to be that the F-86 had a bubble canopy, allowing its pilot much better observation of the fight, and full power hydraulic controls, which is like power steering for fighters.

Although the MiG could, in certain circumstances, turn tighter than the F-86, its heavier controls meant that by the time the MiG pilot had his airplane doing one thing, the F-86 was already doing something else. The MiG's theoretically higher EM performance rarely led to wins in actual or even in practice air-to-air combat.[67]

This caused Boyd a lot of problems, since his reputation in the Air Force as a whole rested on his EM theory. After he retired in 1975, and after much thought, Boyd decided that the F-86 won because it could generate something he called "asymmetric fast transients." A "transient" is a shift from one state[68] to another, "fast" refers to the time it takes to make the shift (not, as is often thought, the velocity of the aircraft itself), and "asymmetric" means that one side is better at it than the other.

An "asymmetric fast transient," though, is not a traditional maneuver done more quickly, even much more quickly. In business, it should not conjure up an image of doing what you're doing now, just doing it faster. The "transient" is the change between maneuvers. In Boyd's concept, the ideal asymmetric fast transient is an abrupt, unexpected, jerky, disorienting change that causes at least a hesitation and preferably plants the seeds of panic in the other side. It's a "What-the f___k!" change in circumstances, and in the interval when the opponent is trying to comprehend what the f___k is, Boyd would strike. What this described vis-à-vis the MiG and the F-86 is that the American fighter could set up novel and unexpected conditions and exploit them before the Russian could react with his sometimes superior EM capability.

It soon became clear that unlike EM, which only describes combat between fighters, fast transients can be found in most any form of competition. Boyd and his colleagues began analyzing war in general and time after time the idea of "asymmetric fast transients," where one side could create and then exploit situations more rapidly than the other, seemed to explain why the winning side won. The great Olympic and professional boxer Muhammad Ali had said virtually the same thing when he described his strategy as "float like a butterfly, sting like a bee."

Boyd inferred that if you can do things before the other side reacts, you can greatly increase your chances of winning, and it doesn't make much difference how big or how strong the other guy is. Asymmetric fast transients, in other words, appeared to do a much better job of explaining real world results than simple counts of weapons or assessments of technology.

It would surprise nobody that you can tip the balance of war if you can hit the other guy and get out before he can hit back, if you cause damage without taking it in return. Boyd went beyond destruction and body counts, however and began to focus on the deteriorating mental state of the slower party. He observed that the quicker side in modern warfare was often able to produce the psychological results of Table I back in chapter II, even before the physical damage had become decisive. The pieces of a new strategy were falling into place.

Agility: Meet the OODA Loop

Our strategic directives were dynamism, initiative, mobility, and rapidity of decision in the face of new situations.[69] Gen Vo Nguyen Giap.

The idea that operating at a quicker time pace than one's opponent can produce psychological effects offers a way out of the "bigger (or more expensive) is better" syndrome. An opponent who cannot make decisions to employ his forces effectively—his command and staff functions become paralyzed by bickering and bureaucracy, for example—is defeated before the engagement begins, no matter how many weapons sit in his inventory. In this way, one could truly achieve Sun Tzu's goal of winning without fighting.

To be useful, though, the new theory needed a concrete representation of abrupt "asymmetric fast transients" outside of the realm of air combat. After examining many wars, battles, and engagements, Boyd synthesized his now well-known "OODA Loop." A participant in a conflict, any conflict, may be thought of as engaging in four distinctive although not distinct activities:

- He must **observe** the environment, which includes himself, his opponent, the physical, mental, and moral situation, and potential allies and opponents.
- He must **orient** himself to decide what it all means. Boyd calls orientation a "many-sided, implicit cross-referencing" process involving the information observed, one's genetic heritage, social environment, and prior experiences, and the results of analyses one conducts and synthesis that one forms
- He must reach some type of **decision**.
- He must attempt to carry out that decision. That is, he must **act**.

Hence the OODA loop. We will spend many pages on OODA loop concepts, but for now, here are a few introductory remarks:

"Observe" means much more than "see." "Absorb" might be more descriptive if it did not have a passive undertone. "Go out and get all the information you can by whatever means possible" is even closer. You can never be sure beforehand which stray idea will provide the key to unlock some fatal dilemma. German strategists recognized that this was as important to the soldier in the foxhole as for a general in his headquarters. As General Hermann Balck, whom Boyd regarded as one of World War II's best field commanders and whose rifle regiment was one of the first across the Meuse during the Blitzkrieg, put it, "The training of the infantryman can never be too many-sided."[70] Musashi, who gave up bathing and other activities generally associated with personal hygiene, still insisted that his disciples be open to all areas of knowledge—that they cultivate the arts in particular—and he produced calligraphy and watercolors that are admired today.

"Orient" is the key to the process. Conditioned by one's genetic heritage, surrounding culture, and previous learning, the mind combines fragments of ideas, information, conjectures, impressions, etc., to form the "many-sided, implicit cross-references," which become a new orientation.

How well your orientation matches the real world is largely a function of how well you observe, since in Boyd's conception, "observe" is the only input from the outside. Like the canopy on the Korean-era MiGs, anything that restricts the inflow of information or ideas can lead to mismatches (disorientations) between what you think is happening and what actually is and may also delay you from spotting (and so acting upon) these mismatches.

Since what you're looking for is mismatches, a general rule is that bad news is the only kind that will do you any good. To thrive in any form of maneuver conflict, you must seek out and find data that don't fit with your current worldview and you must do this while there is still time. Otherwise the world will change—or more likely your adversaries or competitors will change it for you—and you will find yourself disoriented and in the position of playing catch-up. You will have lost the initiative, which is dangerous in any conflict.

In the military, the function of obtaining and understanding information from the outside is called "intelligence." Today, despite a stream of intelligence failures, intelligence is not highly prized in the

United States military establishment. The highest-ranking uniformed officer in charge of a Defense Department intelligence organization wears three stars, one less than the general who runs purchasing and weapons development for the Air Force.[71] This is certainly not the way an organization operating according to Boyd would do things. As Sun Tzu put it in the last chapter of *The Art of War*:

> *No reward is more generous than that for a spy . . . There is nothing for which one cannot employ spies.*[72]

Those who know the situation in the marketplace serve the role of spies for the leaders of modern companies. They will sometimes be bearers of bad news, and, if you follow the Sun Tzu tradition, they will bear this news to you while there is time to act. They are saviors of the company and should be recognized and rewarded as such. True, it takes a strong leader to admit publicly that a position that he or she championed is now wrong or outdated. But in this day and age, companies without strong leaders are doomed, anyway. Those readers who are entering management with the goal of someday sitting in corner offices and receiving the supplications of underlings should put this book down now.

Decisions can transition us into the action stage. For an individual, though, if observe and orient were done well you just know what to do the vast majority of the time. Such "implicit decision making" is another way to look at the notion of "intuitive competence."[73] For groups, explicit decisions, which are how the decision stage of the OODA loop is usually interpreted, can serve to set and when needed to shift the main effort, that is, they can focus and give direction to large numbers of individuals. If, however, you look at Boyd's final version of the OODA loop in the Appendix, you'll see a couple of "Implicit Guidance and Control" arrows, reflecting that most decision making can and should be implicit, and that quite often, orientation controls action directly without the need for explicit decisions at all.

This means that in the OODA concept as Boyd envisioned it, competition is not a simple cycle. This is a critical idea that is often misunderstood: You are *simultaneously* observing any mismatches between your conception of the world and the way the world really is, trying to reorient to a confusing and threatening situation, and attempting to come up with ideas to deal with it. It is the quickness of the entire cycle, and in particular, the time it takes to, in Boyd's language, "transition from one orientation state to another," and not just or even particularly the speed of the O-to-O-to-D-to-A axis, that determines agility and competitive power.[74]

So the most effective visualization of the OODA loop is *not*:

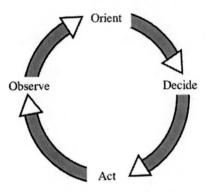

Figure 4—A Common Misconception

but something more like:

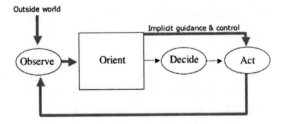

Figure 5—An OODA "Loop" with Power

where the thicker arrows represent the usual and simultaneous flow and the dashed lines are used only when implicit guidance is not adequate. Boyd's final conception of the OODA loop, included in the Appendix, is only slightly more complex.

It bears repeating that if you cannot or do not spot mismatches, and generally this means finding bad news, your orientation becomes detached from reality. Then, since decision and action flow from orientation, your decisions (implicit and explicit) will be flawed and your actions will not have the effects you intend. Furthermore, you won't understand why all this is happening to you, despite your best efforts, and breakdowns at both the group and individual levels can be expected.[75] You will have lost the initiative, and short of sheer dumb luck, you are going to lose the conflict.

What All This Does to the Other Side

> *Business is a dogfight. Your job as a leader: Outmaneuver the competition .... That's why the OODA loop, the brainchild of "40 Second" Boyd, an unconventional fighter pilot, is one of today's most important ideas in battle or in business.*[76]

Boyd got the idea for "O-O-D-A" loops (he used dashes indicate that the steps are not distinct, but flow into each other) from observing the effects of jerky, unexpected, and abrupt maneuvers in air-to-air combat. After deciding that it was his quick OODA loops that allowed him to fight this way, Boyd defined "agility" in these terms: A side in a conflict or competition is *more agile* than its opponent if it can execute its OODA loops more quickly. This generalizes the term *agility* from air-to-air combat and from warfare in general. It also turns out to be equivalent to the definition floated in chapter II, the ability to rapidly change one's orientation, since it is orientation locking up under the stress of competition and conflict that causes OODA loops to slow and makes one predictable, rather than abrupt and unpredictable. Speed, that is physical velocity, may provide an important tactical option, but it is not *The Way*.[77] In fact, speed increases momentum, which can make one more predictable.

What Boyd discovered was that the side with the quicker OODA loops began to exert a strange and terrifying effect on its opponent. Quicker OODA execution caused the slower side to begin falling farther and farther behind events, to begin to lose touch with the situation. Acting like the "asymmetric fast transients" experienced by fighter pilots, these mismatches with reality caused the more agile side to start becoming ambiguous in the mind of the less agile.

Ambiguity is a terrible thing, much more effective as a strategy than deception, with which it is often confused. Deception is correctly described as a tactic: If you are deceived, you will be surprised when you discover the truth, and it is possible that you will be led to do some things, perhaps even fatal things, that you would not have done if you had realized the truth earlier. It can be an extremely effective tactic, even though your ability to function as a thinking human being is not at risk. This is exactly what you can attack and destroy using ambiguity.

Sun Tzu insisted that all warfare is based upon deception. There is no conflict, however, between ambiguity and deception, since the first provides an environment for generating the second. As Brigadier General Samuel Griffith noted in his the introduction to his translation of *The Art of War*: "Sun Tzu realized that an indispensable preliminary to battle was to attack the mind of the enemy"[78] ideally to drive him insane, that is, beyond the ability to operate as a rational human being.

One advances not in the open, for example, where even a massive force can be assessed logically, but by devious and hidden routes, employing feints and disguises. If something vital, such as life itself, is at stake, losing track of a deadly threat in the fog of ambiguity can quickly lead to confusion, panic, and terror (which was the idea behind those Alfred Hitchcock classics), which in turn will cause the decision-making of the less agile party to break down. Deception then becomes like taking candy from a baby, and at this point he can easily be finished off, should that still be necessary.

Friction

"Friction," wrote the 19th century Prussian general and philosopher Carl von Clausewitz, "is the only conception that more or less corresponds to that which distinguishes real war from war on paper."[79] Along with his insistence that "War is the continuation of politics by other means," it is his most famous quote. Yet, it says less than it seems to. The implication is that you analyze war "on paper" (nowadays on a computer) and what you cannot capture there is by definition, "friction." In Boyd's concept of strategy, this misses the whole point. What's inherently important in conflict—such factors as trust, focus and direction, intuitive competence, leading through mission orders, and employing rapid OODA loops to shroud the enemy in a fog of ambiguity and destroy his ability to function—these aren't captured by "war on paper" at all, and it's not a matter of a little "friction" getting in the way.

Oddly, Clausewitz was well aware of many of these same things, and when he describes the *effects* of friction, he and Boyd are not far apart. Clausewitz illustrates friction thorough the simile that doing things in battle is like moving in water. This doesn't sound too bad, but imagine that you are trying to escape from a pursuing sheriff's posse. Hounds are braying; bullets are zinging overhead. Suddenly you run off a bank and plunge into a river. As you thrash around waist deep, you find that the faster you try to go, the harder everything is. Your life depends on moving faster, but you can't, and the harder you try, the more frustrated you get.

It won't take much of this before panic begins to sink in, and you lose the ability to make effective decisions—very much like the effects Boyd and Sun Tzu aim for. They don't come directly from the physical difficulty of moving through water so much as from not knowing how far away the dogs are and from the fact that nothing you're trying seems to be making the situation any better and you're running out of ideas fast. It's not industrial strength ambiguity—you know that there are just dogs out there, although not exactly where, and deputies with shotguns, and you know there are no giant sharks cruising in the muddy water—and so you will probably not descend all the way into blubbering imbecility.

Friction, however, is best discussed in terms of groups of people competing against each other. It arises inevitably from the problems of trying to get people in groups to work together, since under conditions of stress, group dynamics can make the simplest tasks extremely difficult, as Clausewitz observed. But like the Japanese samurai before him, Boyd insisted—and it is a cornerstone of his strategy and a fundamental difference with Clausewitz—that in a competitive situation, friction need not be left to chance. Boyd prescribes active measures to generate and magnify friction in the mind of the opponent, and one good way to do this is through operating at a quicker decision tempo—quicker OODA loops. As ambiguity and frustration grow in the decision-making councils of the slower side, Clausewitz's friction will grow right along with them.

OODA, Friction, and the Blitzkrieg

The Germans, or some small fraction of them, were able to execute and sustain fast decision cycles, even against the friction of war, because they had instilled an organizational climate or culture that mitigated friction's effects. More important in Boyd's view was that by accelerating their OODA loops, they could generate those unexpected, abrupt, and "jerky" transients, such as when they suddenly appeared in force in the south (Map 4), that enabled them to pump up friction on the allied side. It wasn't that the Germans were smarter than the French and British or could peer farther into the future. No, their secret of success lay in that organizational climate, which enabled them to better exploit the chaos that would come, and in fact that they were helping to create.

We will return to this process and apply it to business in chapter V. As a first example of how modern organizations apply the ideas we have been discussing, this chapter will close with a brief look at how the US military have incorporated agility into their doctrines.

Agility in US Military Doctrine

> *The reason we're winning is that we're kind of outthinking him. We're operating inside his decision cycle.*—Brigadier General Richard Neal, US Central Command, Riyadh, Saudi Arabia, February 1991[80]

The Army was the first to put the concept of agility into formal written doctrine. In their Field Manual 3-0, *Operations*, the Army tells its soldiers that:

> *Agility is the ability to move and adjust quickly and easily. It springs from trained and disciplined forces. Agility requires that subordinates act to achieve the commander's intent and fight through any obstacle to accomplish the mission.* (Emphasis in the original)

Operational agility stems from the capability to deploy and employ forces across the range of Army operations. Army forces and commanders shift among offensive, defensive, stability, and support operations as circumstances and missions require. This capability is not merely physical; it requires conceptual sophistication and intellectual flexibility.

Tactical agility is the ability of a friendly force to react faster than the enemy. It is essential to seizing, retaining, and exploiting the initiative. Agility is mental and physical. Agile commanders quickly comprehend unfamiliar situations, creatively apply doctrine, and make timely decisions.[81]

The Army considers initiative practically an object of worship, so you can see what a strong statement this is. On the other hand, they don't bring out the notion that tactical agility is more than the ability to "react faster than the enemy"—nor do they consider the effects a more agile force has on the mind of its opponent. Note that the Army omits the time element from operational agility, making it more like "flexibility" than Boyd's concept of agility.

The Army has made efforts to institutionalize agility in its culture. Before the First Gulf War, the Army established a year-long course, the School of Advanced Military Studies (SAMS) at Ft. Leavenworth, Kansas, where a select group of Command and Staff College graduates study ways to apply warfare based on rapid decision cycles—"maneuver warfare." Boyd worked with SAMS's founder, then-Colonel Huba Wass de Czege, and lectured there on several occasions. SAMS alumni call themselves "Jedi Knights," and Gen Schwarzkopf's staff in Riyadh contained upwards of 60 of them.[82]

Air Force basic doctrine used to take a more sophisticated approach than the Army, or at least what the Army wrote down in its doctrine. Instead of "agility," they called it "timing and tempo," and their 1984 *Basic Doctrine Manual*[83] made it clear what they expected to accomplish:

Timing and tempo allow friendly forces to "dominate the action, remain unpredictable, and create uncertainty in the mind of the enemy."

For a strategist, "create uncertainty" is a powerful concept since it opens possibilities to exploit these uncertainties and create the sort of chaos that Boyd envisioned. The 1996 version of this manual is much more conventional in its thinking, though, and drops the emphasis on "timing and tempo."

Boyd's involvement in USAF strategy and doctrine was limited, and, as Robert Coram related in his biography of Boyd[84], senior Air Force leaders largely ignored his work. Long after his retirement, though, his ideas did enjoy some renaissance at the Air War College, if not in the broader Air Force. He was invited to participate in two Chief-of-Staff-sponsored studies at the War College and he also presented *Patterns of Conflict* and his other briefings there. Professor Grant Hammond, Chair of the Center for Strategy and Technology, interviewed Boyd and many of his associates during these sessions and wrote a biography published in 2001.[85]

The Navy has developed a sophisticated view of agility, particularly as applied to command and control. In *Naval Command and Control* (NDP 6), they state that:

> *However,* the essential lesson of the decision and execution cycle is the absolute importance of generating tempo. *Maintaining rapid decision and execution cycles-and thus a rapid tempo of operations-requires that seniors and subordinates alike have an accurate image of the battlespace and a shared vision of what needs to be done. With this common perspective, commanders are able to experience superior situational awareness and make more effective decisions, enabling them to exercise initiative during combat.*

NDP 6 also describes the OODA loop in some detail and discusses the role of orientation in words reminiscent of Boyd's own. The document, issued in May 1995, established official doctrine for both the Navy and the Marine Corps, and was signed by both the Chief of Naval Operations (the highest ranking officer in the Navy) and the Commandant of the Marine Corps. As in the Army's concept, note the emphasis on initiative.

The most advanced combat doctrine belongs to the US Marine Corps, which is part of the Department of the Navy. Their manual, MCDP1, *Warfighting*,[86] lays out a concept of maneuver warfare entirely consistent with the ideas of agility that we have been exploring:

> *By our actions, we seek to impose menacing dilemmas in which events happen unexpectedly and faster than the enemy can keep up with them* (author's note: asymmetric fast transients) . . . *The ultimate goal is panic and paralysis, an enemy who has lost the will to resist.*"

Thus the Marines subscribe to Musashi's designation of the enemy's spirit as the *Schwerpunkt*. At this point, the battle is won, and all that is left is to march the prisoners off to camp. Boyd worked closely with the originators of Marine maneuver warfare doctrine, particularly the team under Col Mike Wyly that wrote *Warfighting*, and also gave his briefings there on several occasions. The USMC Library at Quantico, Virginia, holds Boyd's archives, and the Commandant at the time of Boyd's death, Gen Charles Krulak, wrote a moving eulogy.[87]

Does it work? Here's what then-Secretary of Defense Cheney told the President and Congress in the first *Annual Report* after the First Gulf War:

> *"The effectiveness of our Marine Corps forces was most dramatically demonstrated by the brilliant movement of I MEF through numerically superior defensive forces into Kuwait City—revalidating the maneuver warfare doctrine adopted by the Corps.*"[88]

As we now know from Robert Coram's book, Secretary Cheney summoned Boyd to Washington several times during Desert Shield (the prelude to the liberation of Kuwait, Desert Storm) and the final version of the plan reflected Boyd's ideas on maneuver warfare.[89]

Agility is a natural concept for the Marines. They form a mobile striking force that aims to get ashore and consolidate a beachhead before the enemy figures out what is going on. An abrupt, unexpected, and disorienting maneuver, much like creating and exploiting a market niche, one might say.

CHAPTER IV

What Strategy Is and
What It Can Do for You

The Americans would be less dangerous if they had a regular army.
British General Frederick Haldimand, Boston, 1776.[90]

Why Strategy?

At the dawn of the 21st century, strategy seems to have gone out of fashion. At the big consulting companies, strategy business is down, while billings for information systems surge. It is as if corporate leaders believe that it is more important to install technology than to understand what to do with it. This is a dangerous attitude since it is possible to spend billions implementing technology that will make the company less competitive, as General Motors did with its automation effort in the 1980s that coincided with its 40% drop in market share.

We have seen that in war, technology has not been a strong factor in determining who wins, whereas strategy is often the difference between victory and defeat:

> *Therefore it is said that victorious warriors win first, then go to war, while defeated warriors go to war first, then seek to win.*[91]

Even our notion of strategy today is tepid compared to what the ancients used. The Homeric Greeks, for example, had the concept of *metis*, which meant "strategy," and also had the connotation of cunning, deception, concealment, ambush and surprise.[92] The complement to *metis* is *bie*, which essentially means "violent force." Both were necessary in battle, but it was Odysseus's *metis* that finally defeated Troy where Achilles's *bie* had failed.

Strategy was not an abstract issue for the Greeks. War was much more a part of their daily lives than for modern Americans and Western Europeans, where war has become something we watch on the evening news or experience as rising prices at the gas pumps. In heroic Greece, if your army lost, your walls were pulled down, surviving male adults killed, and women and children raped and enslaved. So they had a strong incentive to get strategy right, and the concepts they developed, like *metis*, were grounded in objective experience.

The strategies of Sun Tzu also evolved through testing in troubled times, an era so chaotic that it is known to this day as the Warring States Period. In the 2,500 years since Sun Tzu, commentators and practitioners have refined his ideas and added their experiences to account for the evolution of warfare. John Boyd continued this development, addressing the Blitzkrieg and modern guerilla warfare, and it is his formulation that provides the basis of this book.

On Your Own Terms

"If you don't know where you're going," runs a saying I first heard in the Air Force, "any road will take you there." In a competitive environment, not knowing where you're going may well lead you to some place you didn't want to be. Your ultimate purpose is to survive in a threatening and confusing world. But survival *per se* will hardly arouse the passion and commitment you need to win. Prisoners survive. Hostages survive. Your goal is to survive on your own terms, or, echoing Faulkner, to prevail, however you define the term.[93]

Down through history, people who had passively endured conquest and economic privation have turned and fought to their very destruction for ideas. During the early Middle Ages, an itinerant preacher named Peter the Hermit persuaded thousands of peasants to join him in "liberating" the Holy Land. They set out across Europe in 1096, and three years later, the scant few who survived, joined by later contingents of knights, conquered Jerusalem.[94]

So winning requires more than the promise of survival. It must offer an idea of such power and appeal that people will, at times, neglect their other responsibilities and work nights and weekends and extend trips to make it happen.

When discussing the notion of *grand strategy*, Boyd concluded that:

> *What is needed is a vision rooted in human nature so noble, so attractive that it not only attracts the uncommitted and magnifies the spirit and strength of its adherents, but also undermines the dedication and determination of any competitors or adversaries. Moreover, such a unifying notion should be so compelling that it acts as a catalyst or beacon around which to evolve those qualities that permit a collective entity or organic whole to improve its stature in the scheme of things.*[95]

Powerful in war, but can it apply to business? Consider the original Apple ad for the Mac that ran during the 1984 Super Bowl—it helped create a cadre of loyalists that have kept the company alive for 20 more years, despite the fact that for years, Apples were slower and more expensive than comparable PCs from Dell, HP, or IBM.[96] It is not uncommon to read postings on the Mac Internet forums urging people to buy some accessory or software "to help support Apple." Similarly, many people drive the 300 mile roundtrip from my home in Atlanta to Birmingham, Alabama, to fly Southwest Airlines, and it's not unusual for passengers to help the cabin crew pick up trash during their famously short ground times (as I have found myself doing.) The idea is that not only does a compelling mission motivate and uplift employees, but it attracts and keeps customers and sometimes makes them fanatic adherents of the company.

This is the connotation of "survival on your own terms"—people don't put in this amount of effort and passion for somebody else's terms. For this reason, the first task of strategy is to define and win agreement on what "your own terms" really means.

Goals and Visions

These higher purposes are sometimes called "overarching goals"[97] or "unifying vision"[98]. Some businesses have this sense of purpose, above making enough profit to survive, or adding a few more million to the CEO's compensation package. So Alfred Sloan's famous description of General Motors' mission as, "We don't make cars, we make money," worked fine—until his successors faced the Japanese, who made better cars, and, incidentally, lots of money.

There is a risk in all this. You are not the church or the Red Cross or even the government. Your purpose as a business is not to bring enlightenment to humanity but to, as Toyota puts it, "take our destiny into our own hands." It is hypocritical to pretend otherwise, and any attempt to do so will be seen by your employees as the fraud that it is. What you typically find in this situation, as we have all seen, is the "vision statement" that says nothing ("We want to be the best.") or worse, collects a grab bag of trite clichés in one convenient location ("We aspire to empower all our people to achieve their personal goals, while delivering the greatest value proposition to our customers.")

My experience suggests that the reason many companies find it so hard to write vision statements that work is that they have no vision that employees or customers find compelling. Boyd's climate contains an element, the *Schwerpunkt* (focus and direction) that companies can employ to gain the benefits of "vision." They should just go easy on the saccharine "vision statement."

The trick is that your vision can be business oriented, as is Toyota's, and still serve to rally the troops. Close your eyes and imagine what your company should look like. I worked in manufacturing for several years, and some of my most vivid memories are of being too near the door at quitting time. Suppose we changed things. Suppose we made the company such a compelling place to work that when the horn sounded you didn't see anything different right at first. Then people would start filtering out, mostly in groups. Every now and then, the groups would stop, get into excited discussions, and a few people would go back into the plant, furiously gesturing about some problem that couldn't wait.

Although this is not the only possible vision of a winning company—and is actually more a symptom that the company has a real mission than a statement of that mission itself—one whose people have this level of commitment and initiative will be tough to beat. What, specifically, got them all excited? I don't know—it's your business and your industry. Ask yourself what gets you excited (This stuff is usually contagious.)

Strategy

Once we have an idea of where we want to go, we can talk about a strategy to get us there. In a chaotic and dangerous world, strategy fills the gap between our present goals and our future actions. Over the years, people have devised many definitions of strategy. Since you are bound to get into "What is strategy" arguments, every strategist should collect definitions. Here are several to get you started.

From war:

> *The art and science of employing the armed forces of a nation or alliance to secure policy objectives by the application of threat of military force.*
> US Army Field Manual 100-5, Operations, 1986.

> *Victory is achieved in the way of conflict by ascertaining the rhythm of each opponent, by attacking with a rhythm not anticipated by the opponent, and by the use of knowledge of the rhythm of the abstract.*
> Miyamoto Musashi, samurai strategist, 17th century Japan; Nihon Services Group trans.

From business:

> *Strategy is a deliberate search for a plan of action that will develop a business's competitive advantage and compound it.* Bruce Henderson, Founder, the Boston Consulting Group.

> *Strategy isn't beating the competition, it's serving the customer's real needs.* Kenichi Ohmae, Managing Director, McKinsey & Co., Tokyo Office.

From everyday life:

> *The art of the possible in a world where constraints force us to choose between unpleasant or imperfect alternatives.* Retired Pentagon official and long-time Boyd associate Franklin C. Spinney, author of *Defense Facts of Life.*

As you can see, there is no agreement on a general definition, although all contain the idea of achieving some goal. None seem anywhere as powerful as what the ancients demanded from their strategy, although perhaps that goes with the times. The question is whether your concept of strategy will help you win today.

Strategies and Plans

Because the future is unpredictable, a strategy can only be built from intentions: Given where you are now and where you think you want to go, now, what can you do, now, to help you get there? A strategy is not a fact, or a forecast, or a schedule, or a roadmap to the future. Is a strategy, then, a type of plan?

The two concepts are often confused, since plans deal with the future and so does strategy. We could regard strategy as simply an offshoot of planning, as the Army definition suggests in the collection above. However, as Scottish poet Robert Burns observed about the best laid ones of mice and men,[99] plans are poor tools for dealing with uncertainty, ambiguity, and confusion—what distinguishes real business from business on paper (or in a computer.)

Even during Operation Desert Storm, which many people regard as a walkover, Schwarzkopf and his commanders took strategy seriously and made five major adjustments to their plans. Some of these were fundamental, such as the shift of the major attack hundreds of miles to the west, whereas others exploited the opportunity of the moment, such as beginning the VII Corps' assault on the Republican Guard on the second, rather than the third day of the ground attack.

In the Second Gulf War, General Tommy Franks and his subordinate commanders made the decision to launch the ground war ahead of the air campaign on less than one day's notice, thereby achieving operational surprise and preempting damage to the southern Iraqi oil fields. In both cases, they did not make changes capriciously. There were overall guiding frameworks—strategies—to the battles that gave the coalition commanders bases for the changes to their plans.

Bruce Henderson, in the definitions above, related plans to strategies but defined strategy as the search and the plan as the result. Like Henderson, I am going to draw a distinction between the two concepts, and consider a plan as something more specific than a strategy. A **plan** is an intention about how to get from where we are now to where we want to be in the future. It is an intention because although we may plan to accomplish certain things, whether we actually do, and whether they have the effects we want, depends on factors beyond our control: customers, competitors, governments, and acts of God, to name a few. The term **strategy** will be used for higher-order devices for creating and managing plans.

In business as in war, we need higher-order concepts that will give us a competitive advantage when things go awry, knowing with certainty that they will. To construct such a device, let's create a crude model of the planning process.

Plans are what we intend to do to get from *Now* to where we want to be in the *Future*. To build a specific a plan, we have to make assumptions about what the future will bring. In other words, we have to construct a **scenario**. We can represent one such plan, with its embedded scenario, as a simple arrow[100]:

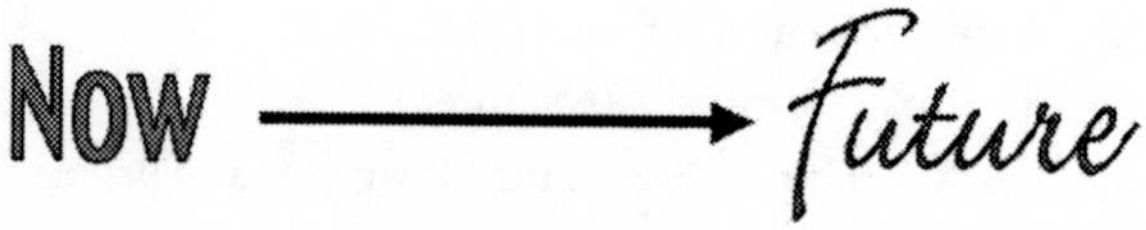

Now ——————▶ *Future*

Figure 6—A Single Plan

In real life, unpredictable actions by customers and competitors ensure that things don't often work out exactly according to plan. For example, our original plan, which we'll call Plan A, might have called for us to develop a certain device in-house. Of course, that scenario might not happen, that is, we might not be able to develop it ourselves in the time required, or a competitor might bring out a better one while ours is still in development. Therefore, we might consider an alternative scenario, and an associated (back-up) Plan B, to divert additional budget to the project and accelerate advanced features (for example) if we get leapfrogged by the competition:

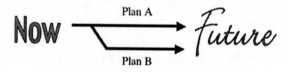

Figure 7—Planning For (a Little) Uncertainty

Likewise, we might have Plans C and D, which account for other possibilities:

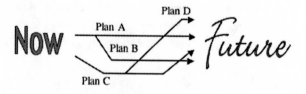

Figure 8—The Real World Intrudes

Similarly, we might have alternative goals, Future1, Future2, Future3. If our R&D effort succeeds soon enough, we might try to push the competition with a radical new approach, saving our original design as a hedge or a lower-priced, entry-level version. As a general rule, it is not a good idea to bet the company on a single vision of the future. At this stage, our planning process looks something like this:

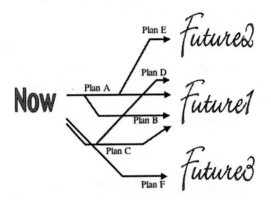

Figure 9—Is the Cure Worse Than the Problem?

If you keep this process up, you will discover two things. First, you will spend a lot of time trying to map out the future: "If this happens, I'll do that. On the other hand, if that happens, I'll do this. On the third hand . . ." You might want to add a fortuneteller or a prophet to your staff. At the same time you'll discover that these models, which are a type of "decision tree," quickly become complex. Instead of helping you deal with the confusion of the world, this approach can easily add to it.

Isn't it true that even if you stopped right here, overcome by the proliferating futures, arrows, and "what ifs," the process (as distinguished from the final plan itself) will probably have done some good? Your organization will have thought about the basics of your business—the objectives, customers, competitors, skills, and technologies that make you what you are. While nobody can argue that these are not important, strategy demands more. Do you believe that you can create a plan for every eventuality? Each scenario will suggest ten more, and you will soon wrap yourself in a web of nodes and arrows from which you will never escape, and you will have to pay in money and time for the effort. Perhaps most important: where is the antidote to confusion and chaos? The idea behind strategy is to create chaos in the opponent, not in ourselves.

There is a way to preserve the benefits of planning while avoiding the prophetic nature and the complexity of formal decision models and which will also help you exploit the chaos of the real world. You can use strategy to give this process a shape that the human mind can work with. What type of strategy will do this? The basic idea revolves around the notion of "focus and direction" that we discussed in chapter III, a device for adding the cohesion that the decision tree so obviously needs.

Thus designating something to give our actions focus and direction, we might look at our world like this:

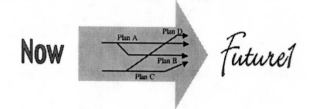

Figure 10—A Strategy, Not Just a Plan

What this says is that *Future1* is the idea of the future that best defines what we want for ourselves and our strategy gives enough guidance for us to construct plans to achieve it. At the level of strategy, we don't worry too much about the specific plans inside the big arrow. We are confident in our abilities to create plans, within the overall strategy, because we have worked and trained together in the past in circumstances not too dissimilar from where we are now. Once Schwarzkopf had the concept of holding the Iraqis in Kuwait and hooking around them to the left, his planning staff and subordinate commanders could do their jobs and create, modify, and discard specific plans.

It is also possible to have multiple plans operating at the same time, within an overall strategy. You can then reinforce the ones that succeed and cut off the ones that don't. This is analogous to an important concept in maneuver warfare known as "multiple thrusts" that we will examine near the end of chapter V.

As a part of strategy distinct from managing plans, we also keep an eye on the alternative visions of the future, *Future2* and *Future3*. At some point, largely determined by our judgment and experience, our intuitive feel for the situation, we might shift the main focus. We might, to take one possibility, sense that customer preferences are changing (for example, due to products that have been introduced while our project was in development or to the changing economic environment) from what we originally expected, and so we make a shift in the market niche we are aiming for. IBM's shift of focus from hardware to services or Intel's from memory chips to microprocessors represent two examples. At this point, once we have shifted the main focus, we will begin constructing new plans in harmony with it.

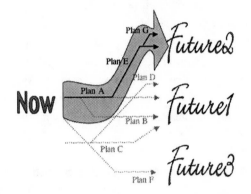

Figure 11—Using Strategy To Exploit Chaos and Complexity

Strategy, then, includes selecting the view of the future we want, creating devices to harmonize all the plans and actions designed to achieve that future, and on relatively rare occasions, shifting to an alternate future.

A Definition

We can work all this into a formal definition by incorporating several of the concepts we have already discussed. The most basic concern of any strategy is to increase our ability to survive on our own terms in a threatening and confusing world. Because companies and armies are both groups of people, strategy should serve to harmonize the efforts of individuals in their attempts to deal with this world. If we add the notion that strategies are made up of intentions, not realities, then we have **Boyd's definition:**

> *Strategy is a mental tapestry of changing intentions for harmonizing and focusing our efforts as a basis for realizing some aim or purpose in an unfolding and often unforeseen world of many bewildering events and many contending interests.*[101]

Creating Strategy

This raises the questions of how to create a strategy and what does the "tapestry" look like? This is not a "how-to" manual. In fact, even attempting to create a step-by-step approach would contribute to rigidity and defeat the real purpose of strategy. Still, it seems reasonable that before we create a strategy for business, we should spend some time thinking about what purpose we want it to serve—a "vision," in other words. Although your answer to this question will differ from mine, here is a strawman to get you started:

What a Business Strategy Should Do

- Keep our focus on the customer, with an eye to the competition and the rest of the strategic environment
- Provide our team with a continuing stream of options
- Enable rapid switching between options
- Encourage initiative at all levels—in particular, an execute-and-communicate ("shoot and scoot") mindset rather than one of ask-and-wait
- Harmonize our efforts to achieve the future we have in mind.

Options mean more than new products and services. The creators of the Toyota Production System stress the importance of creating a company culture that constantly reduces costs, as a natural part of daily operations, while improving quality and shortening customer delivery span times. By keeping costs on a steady downward slope, they preserve pricing options, that is, they can reduce prices when economic times are bad and still make a profit. Thus they survive on their own terms, without placing themselves at the mercy of creditors. When times are good, they make money faster than they can count.

A Concept of Strategy for Business

Any strategy must harmonize internal and external considerations, that is, we must align what we intend to accomplish with regard to customers and competitors with our internal capabilities and constraints as they are now but more important, as we can make them during the time interval under consideration. This brings up another difference between strategy and planning: A plan says, "Here's what I intend to accomplish, here's what I've got to work with, so here's what I'm going to do." Strategy can also ask, "Who said this is what I've got to work with? I can develop or buy new capabilities or partner with those who have them." You can talk about "core competence planning," but the expression "core competence strategy" is a *non sequitur* or at least unduly limiting.

Here is an idea for such a strategy. It is certainly not the only one, but it is based on the patterns of thought described so far in this book, and it has worked well for military leaders over the ages:

1. Within your team (company, division, or whatever defines "we" for you), form a clear (though not rigid) view of what "survival on your own terms" means.
2. Cultivate an organizational climate, such as the one described in this book, that will enable your business to operate at increasingly quicker OODA loop speed.
3. Foster an organizational ethos that grows and strengthens the climate, that promotes those who use it and removes those who do not.

This does not just set strategy on a cultural foundation. Rather, the actions you take to create and grow a competitive culture form an inseparable part of your strategy, and you should not view these social aspects in isolation from the rest of strategy.

That these "pre-conflict" activities form an integral part of strategy is an ancient idea. As we saw, the Chinese of Sun Tzu's day insisted that the war was won or lost before the action began, and much of the *Art of War* concerns preparing a culture that is certain to win. Pre-war activities and decisions also form part of the level of conflict known as **grand strategy**—pumping up our morale and attracting the uncommitted to our side. Since in business, "attraction" is the only tool we have to influence customers, there is no essential difference between "business strategy" and "business grand strategy." Yet another distinction between business and war.

Some readers may be uncomfortable with a concept of strategy that does not look like a super-plan (or as one client once told me, a "fuzzy plan."). Although this may take some getting used to, the idea that strategy is something other than a process or the result of a process (e.g., a plan), has been used by successful leaders since people started writing about strategy.

The Chinese, in their commentary on Sun Tzu, summarized the practice of strategy as a way to respond to changing conditions and create timely options. The strategy is in the responding and creating (what OODA loops do), and not in the options (e.g., plans & tactics) themselves. One can almost hear the exasperation in the commentators' voices as they asked how one could possibly say in advance what their specific actions would be. By the late 19th Century, military leaders, driven by the lethality new technology was bringing to the battlefield, realized the need to return to this more flexible and opportunistic view of strategy. Helmuth von Moltke, whose armies had won the wars that unified Germany, concluded that, "Strategy is a system of ad hoc expedients."[102]

Armed with this view of strategy, a few military leaders began to explore alternatives that eventually led to the Blitzkrieg—ways of operating that encouraged initiative on the part of subordinates to flow around lethal threats and search for advantage elsewhere. We have seen the results.

A Strategy of Agility

. . . then break the enemy formation into meaningless chunks that didn't know what they were doing . . . the way they fought seemed like the only intelligent way . . . the only possible way. Orson Scott Card, Ender's Game.[103]

Quick OODA loops will allow you to better track your environment. In particular, you will be able to tuck-in tighter under your customers' wings, and more rapidly discover their needs and wants and respond to them. An agile company can also track changes in customer preferences better than its slower competitors, since it will bring in data from the world (cycle through the observe and orient phases) more often during any period of time.

While these are effects of agility, they represent the passive component. Under this paradigm, there is always a lag: the customer has needs and some time later, you discover them. To turn this into an active tool of strategy, you should ask yourself where these needs and wants come from. Too often they represent successful attempts by competitors to shape the marketplace—customers "want" something because a competitor has offered it to them. Every government and many commercial requests for proposal, for example, contain a "statement of work" (SOW) describing in some detail what the customer wants. The question is, who wrote the SOW?

If you didn't or at least if you didn't have a strong influence upon it, the chances are good that one of your competitors did. That competitor certainly knows what the customer wants better than you do. Similarly in the wider marketplace, customers often want things because competitors have dangled them in their faces. In either case, such "discovery of customer wants" does not provide the basis for strategy; it represents a failure of strategy.

Another reason why discovering customer "wants" may not generate much in the way of useful strategy is that what customers often want is magic—something like IBM's "server pixie dust" in their 2003 commercials, or unlimited free energy, or instant cures of pains and aches, with no side effects. Anyway, it's not their job to do your product development for you, so you have no right to complain if they want things that are impossible under the known laws of physics.[104]

So passive even if rapid trolling for customer "wants" is not going to make you very competitive. Much more interesting to strategists is what agility can do to the mind of a slower competitor. Boyd's graphic description comes back: "generate uncertainty, confusion, disorder, panic, chaos, . . . to shatter cohesion, produce paralysis, and bring about his collapse."

Companies have produced these effects in their competitors, and so can you, but it is still not enough. While reports of feuding may make for entertaining reading in business publications, you have wasted your efforts unless the customer also buys your product instead of your competitors'. So in business, we look to agility to have a two-fold purpose: Keep the competition off balance *while also leading both us and the customer into new ways of conceiving the product or service.* This is what "shaping the marketplace" means. The good news is that it works, and in fact is exactly what Honda did in the H-Y War described in chapter I, where it made newness *per se* a desirable feature.

The best Japanese carmakers routinely use their superior OODA loop speeds both to find and to shape what customers really want, whether the customers know it or not. The Japanese even have a name for it: *miryoku teki hinshitsu,* which roughly translates as "What the customer finds so beguiling or fascinating that he cannot live without it."[105] It is an abrupt change in the customers' attention, from the quality and value they expected to something special and delightful that took them by surprise. This is an analogy of the jarring, unorthodox, and disorienting changes typical of Boyd-type strategies in armed conflict, except that in business, the decisive effect is on the customer, where it counts. We will explore this phenomenon in chapter VI.

Notice that 'shaping the market" is different from a "first mover advantage." The company that introduces a radically new product may not be the one that reaps the most profit—think of Apple with the Newton.[106] Often the first mover—the one who invents the product or service—loses to a competitor who improves it, packages and supports it better, or establishes its version as a standard, as when the VHS video tape format replaced the technically superior Betamax. What I'm talking about is more like a "rapid thinker" advantage that at each moment learns from and influences the marketplace, extracts profits, then moves on before the competition figures it out.

A Simple Example of Agility

Go find the best chess player you can and offer to play for $1,000 under the following conditions:

- Your opponent moves first.
- You move twice for every move of his or hers.

In fact, you can even offer to give up some pieces, to make it more fair. You will find that, unless you are playing somebody at the grandmaster level, you can give up practically everything and still win. Keep the knights and maybe a rook.

This is a graphic illustration of how the smaller side, using agility, can overcome a large disadvantage in numbers. Does it strike you as farfetched and removed from what happens in the real world? Consider that Honda and Toyota can bring out a new model in roughly 2 years, with superb quality, while it still takes Detroit at least a year longer.

Entropy and Other Strange Effects

The truly strange and exciting effects of agility go far beyond the chess game analogy, where everybody can see what the other side is doing. In war, where the situation is never this clear, unexpected and abrupt maneuvers by the more agile side often cause the less agile side to start doing dumb things, a few of which are shown below.[107]

Signs Your Strategy Is Working In War

- Vehicles or couriers blundering into your lines
- You reach an enemy position to find rations still being cooked
- Shelling of your last position after you left

- Surrender after token resistance
- Piles of uniforms by the side of the road
- More prisoners than your military police can handle

As the battle progresses, the slower side's orientation, its mental picture of what is happening, becomes less and less accurate. Recall Liddell Hart's observation on the French in 1940, "their timing was too slow to catch up with the changing situations," and it caused their ability to make decisions to break down.

There is a well-known name for this detachment from reality that strikes the less agile side: *the fog of war.* Boyd's observations on the effects of agility boil down to the conclusion that by becoming more agile than your competitors, you can cause the fog of war to grow in their minds, thereby decreasing the quality of their decisions and eventually attacking their abilities to make effective decisions altogether.

A similar effect, a breakdown in the quality of energy, is well known to students of physics as "entropy." The energy is still there, but it isn't available for doing work. The insidious thing about entropy is that within a closed system, it always increases. In other words, closed systems run down.

In a competitive situation, the less agile competitor will begin to act like a closed system and the fog of war, or the fog of business, for that matter, begins to grow within. And fog plus menace, as Boyd often noted, is a good formula for generating frustration and eventually, panic.

Clausewitz, as you may recall from chapter III, concluded that war generates effects that act like friction, to slow down even the simplest activities. In business as in war, superior agility by one competitor magnifies friction in the slower side. As your strategy begins to work, events will correspond less and less to your competitor's expectations, and frustration compels its members to spend more and more time focused internally, pointing fingers, spreading blame, and grasping at straws.

Ernest Hemingway put a description of this frustration into his great war novel, *A Farewell To Arms.* After one particularly bad defeat, the Italians screened all their retreating soldiers, and executed any Italian officers they found above the rank of captain. Did wonders for Italian morale—not that we, of course, would ever do anything like that in business.

How to Tell It's Working in Business

Unfortunately, I have no eyewitness account of what went on in Yamaha's executive suites during the latter stages of the H-Y War, related in chapter I. I suspect it didn't differ greatly from Joseph Juran's classic description of what happens to a company that is starting to lose:

> *"Lacking victories over their competitors, and unable to defend themselves from their bosses, they lash out at each other, making unity of purpose even harder to achieve."*[108]

This is the business version of what results from a successful Boyd-style operation: "pull adversary apart, produce paralysis, and collapse his will to resist." Boyd notes that by being more agile, you can fold your competitor in on himself so that he complains, like Jack Welch, former chairman of General Electric, that "This internal focus has wasted our time, wasted our energy, frustrated us, made us so mad some nights over some bureaucratic jackass boss that we'd punch a hole in the wall."[109]

How to Tell Your Strategy Is Working in Business

- Your competitor's new products are consistently late and lack your features or quality.
- He starts blaming the customer, or insisting that his sales force "educate the customer."
- Personnel turnover is high.
- He becomes even more "Theory X," instituting rigid, explicit controls, frequently in the name of containing costs.
- He launches witchhunts and other ever-intensifying internal searches for "the cause of the problem."

The cost-cutting fiat is a clear sign. As Tom Peters points out, it is almost impossible to simply "cut costs" without also cutting out some service to the customer or damaging what little of your own morale that remains.[110] This is why companies using the Toyota Production System have an advantage, since year after year they improve their cost, quality, and production time postures, simultaneously.

The best way you can tell your strategy is working is when customers begin to desert your competitors to buy your products and services instead, and competitors' responses indicate that somehow they don't seem to catch on.

Some Strategic Traps

In the previous section, the idea was to bring about the collapse of your competitor by operating at a higher decision cycle speed—that is, with higher agility—thus generating mismatches between your competitor and the customer. In other words, we helped him become a victim of his own poor strategy.

Now, let's turn the problem around. What are some things that can get you into strategic trouble?

First, there is the *Basic Rule of All Competition (BRAC)*: You are not smarter than either the customer or the competition. Mathematically,

$$IQ_{ours} \leq IQ_{theirs}$$

This is why "roadmaps of the future" that masquerade as strategy will get you into trouble. You've seen them: first we're going to do this, then that, then the other thing. As if neither the customer nor competition much mattered. As we have discussed, these are complex plans, that is, intentions, and not strategy at all.

Another trap, also related to BRAC, is rigidity. Formal planning processes seem especially susceptible. There is nothing wrong with planning, and your strategy, as described in this chapter, will generate and discard many of them as you cycle within your OODA loops. Problems can arise if you have a formal planning process with an attendant, enforcing bureaucracy. With all this investment, there is a tendency to take the output of the process (the plans) too seriously, locking you into the plan as the real world goes on its way.

In one company I worked with, managers spent a couple of weeks every year in a detailed numerical evaluation against the objectives in their year-old plan. They used the plan as a checklist. All the various objectives were numbered and they went through them, one-by-one, each manager presenting evidence to show that s/he had indeed met his or her parts of the plan. Nobody raised the issue of how well they helped shape their marketplace. There was no discussion of whether their culture was becoming more competitive, or for that matter, about the competition at all.

To think that you can predict what needs to be done a year from now is sheer arrogance.

A Web of Detail

Oddly, some of the common techniques of modern management can also hamper your strategy. We touched on this point at the end of chapter II, but here is a more concrete example. Figure 12 is typical of the modeling approach to inventory management.

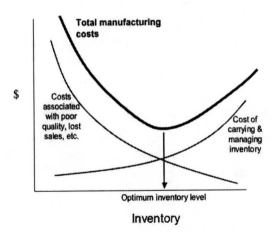

Figure 12—Mathematically Correct, But Wrong

What's wrong with this? Nothing, as research; everything, as strategy.

While we were deriving complex equations for managing inventory, and installing expensive control systems to implement them, Toyota was figuring out ways to do away with it all together (or pretty much).

The result is the famous just-in-time production system. In the conventional system, still widely used in US factories, we build the parts of a product in batches, called "lots." If we need, say, ten parts, we'll build 11 (for example), so that when we need a part, we can usually find a good one. As you can see, this entirely sensible system also institutionalizes waste: It's OK to build poor quality—we even plan on it. When you look at such a system this way, you can see why we have such a difficult time producing world-class products.

What is obviously needed is a method of production where it is not acceptable to produce even one bad or unneeded item. That is the philosophy behind lean production, where something is produced only when it is needed for the next stage of production. And when you look at the data on manufacturing performance, that is what you find. According to studies at MIT, just-in-time is indeed the only system that actually produces significant increases in productivity, and the quality it produces is legendary.[111]

In this case, competitive advantage comes not from better ways to handle inventory, but from fundamental changes that enable a goal of abolishing it altogether.[112] This is an exact analogy to the military case, in which conventional strategy glossed over the factors that actually produce victory, like cohesion/trust, agility, initiative, and the ability to generate surprise and confusion, and instead considered only numbers and weapon effectiveness.

Another, and more insidious strategic effect of complex methodologies is that they can turn the attention of the company inwards. Most of them, for example, require extensive input. A decision methodology that I saw in one company was designed to rate potential investment opportunities. To evaluate 25 prospects, the system needed 225 inputs. Senior managers would spend hours locked up in meetings arguing over these numbers, on whether the probability of a customer responding to a potential new feature, for example, was .42 or .53, and this for something that wouldn't happen for several years. Mostly, of course, they were trying to ensure that programs in their area received high enough priority to get funded. As a result, the attention of management turned inward for weeks at a time during these exercises. It didn't build much unity, trust, or cohesion, either.

If this sort of thing continues, the company culture begins to accept it as the normal way of doing business. People spend weeks getting ready to defend the input numbers that will support their favorite programs. Rather than quick decision cycles about things important to customers, the focus of the company's efforts turn to internal politics and creative justification.

Meanwhile, what about the competition? A few weeks may not sound like much, but the world standard of competition is less and less forgiving of time spent working the wrong problem. Consider that in many industries, such as consumer electronics, the best companies can design and introduce new products in six months or so.

Lessons Learned

Our last strategic trap is a little different, since it doesn't flow directly from intellectual arrogance. It is known as the "lessons learned" syndrome, or, as the military puts it, "fighting the last war." This is the tendency to make major changes to your strategy based primarily (or only) on the last experience you had. One of the reasons we had so much trouble in Vietnam was that the vast majority of our forces were designed to refight WW II, this time against the Soviets, on the plains of Europe.

This sort of thing is also common in business. For example, suppose, for whatever reason, you decide to diversify into handheld microwave cookers. You whip up everybody's enthusiasm, develop and build the product, and then the first one bombs. What do you do? In many companies, the temptation would be to conduct a witch hunt, punish the guilty (and, I suppose, a lot of the innocent), while those who can plausibly adopt an "I told you so" stance rise to the top.

Why did your product fail? In a way, it's a fruitless question since most new products fail in the sense that they don't make back enough money to repay the cost of capital. Both computers and copy machines had to survive early "it will never sell" verdicts by market researchers, but they seem to have done all right. Boyd's view of strategy allows a company to deal with this situation.

If you really believe that the world needs a lightweight, portable, rapid cooking device (this is a vision of the future and a potential *Schwerpunkt*), then trust your instincts, learn what you can from your customers about the first experiment, and press on. If you are right, then maybe it will be you, and not the Japanese, who bring out the first commercially successful version. If not, then if you know your business, your intuition—your Fingerspitzengefühl—will tell you when its time to shift to something else. In any case, the experience will have added to your store of intuitive competence in your field. When Apple was trying to move upscale from the Apple II, it brought out not one, but two commercial flops (the Apple III and the Lisa) before hitting pay dirt with the Mac. It was Steve Jobs' clear focus on an "insanely great" new personal computer that saved Apple from destruction.

There is nothing wrong with conducting post-mortem investigations into your success and failures and you should do this as a matter of course. Problems arise when you change strategies after every one. Management theorists call this tendency to chase the last data point the "Nelson Funnel."[113]

Imagine that you are trying to drop a small ball bearing from a couple of feet up to hit a mark on a tabletop. This is analogous to a plan—the bearing goes from where your hand is, representing "now" to the mark, which represents the future. There is a catch—you have to look down at the mark through a funnel that is maybe twice the diameter at the end of the tube as the bearing. You shoot at the mark by putting the ball into the large end, where it rolls around before coming out the tube at some random time, angle, and angular velocity. This adds an element of unpredictability, as in a real planning process.

The first strategy that comes into most peoples' minds is also the wrong thing to do: observe where the first ball lands—an inch to the right, for example—conduct a post-mortum, and then move the funnel an inch to the left, repeating the process at every step. Under the best of circumstances, and assuming you always keep the mark in view, you will waste a lot of energy in a random walk around the mark. However if you run into a streak of bad luck, or if your timing is off a little so that you start overcompensating, or even become nervous and start shaking the end of the tube, you can lose the mark and wander aimlessly around the table.

The correct procedure is to keep your hand steady with the funnel lined up over the mark at all times, and don't react to the random fluctuations induced by the funnel or your hand. Breathe evenly. Relax. As time goes on, that is, as you accumulate experience, you may be able to discern patterns in how the ball is landing. If you suspect the funnel is introducing biases, moving the ball slightly to the right on average, for example, you can run statistical tests to see if this is true, and then make an adjustment to the funnel—move it the correct amount in the opposite direction, as determined by the results of your tests. As long as you're sure that you're aiming at a mark you want to hit, this is the correct strategy. Unlike many of the numerical techniques I've criticized in this book, this approach represents a valid use of numbers in decision-making.

Keeping your funnel lined up on the mark is analogous to setting a focus and direction. The individual drop points are like the individual plans governed by the strategy. Now suppose the mark also moves every now and then, usually smoothly and continuously, but occasionally jumping quickly to another point. This is how the real world works, after all. Quick OODA loops allow you to confirm whether the mark has actually moved or whether it's only normal hand movement. The more often you're sampling, that is, dropping balls and observing the results, the quicker you will be able to detect real movement by the mark. Reorienting, which is the essence of agility, occurs when you interpret the data to conclude that you have a systemic bias or that the mark has moved and so you have to shift the funnel accordingly.

We can milk even more from this simple analogy. How would you improve your performance? You might decide that the hole at the end of the tube is too big, that what you need is tighter control, in other words. This may seem to work, so you reduce the opening even further. At some point, the passage of the ball through the tube is going to block your view of the mark and normal vibrations in your hand can cause your now tightly focused funnel to lose the mark before you notice anything. To cure this, you might install high technology detecting and reporting mechanisms to try to hold the funnel rigidly in place.

All this might work, until the mark moves. Then it is quite likely that your rigid, top-down (for that is what it is) control mechanism will not be able to track it, or there will be a sizable delay until you realign your control mechanism and recapture the aim point. Plus there's always the possibility that political factions have built up within the organization you've constructed to control the funnel and that they will resist moving the funnel until it is too late—like armies that always want to refight the last war. Or the complex funnel control device could break at an inopportune moment.

There is a principle of strategy that says that when your strategies start becoming aggradations, where each new feature is intended to correct problems found with earlier versions, then it's time to throw the whole thing out and start over.

What if the problem is with the idea of top down control? Why don't we give the ball bearings themselves some amount of initiative to make corrections if they see they're going to miss the mark, like the "smart munitions" the military uses? We can also ask that they communicate back to us what's going on as they drop and where they hit. Then we can dismantle the elaborate control mechanism and the engineers and bureaucracy that support it. We can also loosen up on the opening at the end of the funnel, since we want a certain amount of variation to be able to detect when the mark has moved—if our pattern is too tight, the mark might move out of the range our "smart bearings" can handle and so escape forever.

Giving bearings initiative and asking them to communicate, particularly if they see they're going to miss, may seem farfetched, but it is no problem at all for human beings. The initiative we give the bearings corresponds to managing through missions, rather than tasks, and there is a focus—hit the mark. Once we trust the bearing (and this is stretching the analogy as far as I dare) we leave the details of how to hit it largely up to the bearing itself.

Dr Jonathan Shay, who studies trust and cohesion for a living, once noted that:

*The machine metaphor of a military unit was **never** apt, especially in a fight—where it counts. When you replace the carburetor of a car, it works from the get-go, if it's the right part. It doesn't have to practice stopping and starting with the brake linings, or learn the job of the brake linings so that the brakes and the carburetor say they can read each other's minds. This is the way members of a tight military unit speak of each other.*[114]

The only thing that keeps this analogy from being more exact is that Boyd insisted that by employing trust, focus, mission, and intuitive competence we not only arrive at a future we find acceptable, but we can move the future to where we want it to be, that is, we can also affect when and how the mark moves. We can "herd" it as we train it and it, of course, trains us. The important thing to remember in all of this is that competitors are playing the game, too. If you are not quick enough, the mark may abruptly and unexpectedly vanish.

CHAPTER V

A Climate for Winning in Business

Man is the child of custom, not the child of his ancestors. Arab historian
Ibn Khaldun (1377 A.D.)[115]

Why Culture Is Fundamental

In the previous chapters, I tried to convince you that physical
characteristics, such as size and spending levels, do not guarantee
victory in any highly competitive situation. In war, we have seen smaller
sides win time after time, perhaps most spectacularly in Vietnam and
Afghanistan. In business, we have seen the Japanese come from
devastation to defeat Detroit at its own game on its own turf, and
upstarts like Dell and Southwest Airlines continue to grow at the expense
of their long-established rivals.

Herb Kelleher, chairman and recently retired CEO of Southwest
Airlines, brags that competitors could copy the details of his system—
direct (as opposed to hub-and-spoke) routings, no reserved seats or
meals, one type of aircraft, etc.—but they couldn't copy the culture,

the vibrant esprit de corps, because "they can't buy that."[116] So far his words have been prophetic, at least as far as the other US major airlines are concerned.

Your organization needs such an environment—a culture—that will enable your people to execute rapid OODA loops, and for the rest of this chapter, we will explore one of these, the one introduced back in chapter III as the "Key Attributes of the Blitzkrieg."

Create Mutual Trust

Chapter III described four qualities, with roots down through history, that help an organization run at fast OODA tempo. The first of these is unity, cohesion, oneness, or, as I shall use in the rest of this book, mutual trust between the members of the organization. The German word *Einheit* conveys all these meanings, and I'll use it occasionally as well. Unless you are constantly on guard, "trust," as with any other unalloyed good, will degenerate into a platitude suited only to pronouncements of the company's high mission. Mutual trust, however, really is the foundation for everything that follows, and successful businesses have found ways to make the concept live.

What Mutual Trust Can Do for You

Mutual trust is the internal harmony that converts a mob into a team. For this reason, it underlies all the other components of a competitive organizational climate. It defines the boundary between "us" and "them." We have seen its power to win wars, and it exerts a similarly profound effect in other human endeavors. Everybody seems to recognize this: Magazines like *Fortune*, *Business Week*, and *Fast Company* often feature cover stories on trust and bemoan its erosion in American businesses.[117]

Those modern samurai, the best Japanese industrialists, tell us exactly the same thing. Shigeo Shingo, one of the architects of Toyota's magnificent system, wrote, "I believe the most important factor is maintaining a relationship of trust between labor and management."[118] He goes on to say that the entire foundation of the Japanese system rests on a belief that it is possible to achieve this atmosphere of mutual trust, albeit like the German conception, through working hard together.

Why It Works

Although "mutual trust" gives us all a soft, warm feeling, how does it actually help win? Simply, it speeds execution of OODA loops. The reason? For starters, it permits implicit communication among team members, where very little needs to be written down. Obviously, people can communicate this way much faster than through any form of writing—it's much quicker not to say something than to spell it out in detail. Implicit communication, with enough mutual experience, can provide more information more accurately as well. A raised eyebrow, a subtle change in inflection, a barely-noticed hesitation—these mean something if you have worked together long enough to read them. You learn when the boss is speaking rhetorically and when s/he is really serious, where you can improvise and where you'd best stick to the straight-and-narrow. And this wealth of information transmits in an instant, but only implicitly. On the other hand, explicit forms are often used not to communicate but to document, not to inform but to protect oneself. You may have been in organizations where everybody documented everything. My guess is that you did not notice much trust.

Mutual trust / cohesion is unique among harmonizing agents in that it encourages individual initiative. This point is worth stressing because as we all know, there are ways to achieve, perhaps better would be "enforce," a sort of harmony by eliminating initiative. This is unfortunate because by establishing and then relying on trust, you can have harmony and initiative, too. People are much more likely to seek initiative in a climate of trust than in a climate of fear, which is at least one benefit of Deming's command to "Drive out fear!" And of course, initiative, which means seeking out and doing it now, not waiting for permission, is essential for quick OODA loops.

Ethics

Ethics is in fashion in the post-Enron world. Defense contractors, for example, require their employees to take four or so hours of annual "ethics training." Everybody troops in, watches the films, signs the roll, and leaves. Then throughout the year, management can certify that if there is evidence of misconduct, their hands are clean.

In the hard-nosed world of modern business, is there a purpose to ethics? Or is it just "good" as in "good PR"? Although high ethical standards should be their own reward, ethics actually provides a powerful competitive force. Why? Ethics fosters trust, which is why business ethics does more than simply provide a cozy feeling for management. Consider this: We've all worked with people who took delight in what they could do to suppliers or customers even under circumstances when it was strictly legal. Did you trust them?

One of my favorite pictures from the Era of Greed appeared on the cover of the March 2002 *Business 2.0*. It shows Kenneth Lay, then-chairman of Enron (no longer billing itself as "The World's Greatest Company") with a Pinocchio nose and the headline: "Liar!" Quite a way to be remembered by posterity.

How to Get It

Mutual trust comes from mutual experience. You have seen how a group of people who put in a month of 20-hour days to meet a deadline, especially one that first seemed impossible, develop a special relationship that lasts long after the project is over. During this process, the members of the team also form common orientations that encourage implicit— and so extraordinarily rapid-communication. It is what the military tries to create during basic training.

The strategic effect, the impact on customers and competitors, of mutual trust is faster company OODA loops. There are even strong benefits in those parts of your operation that have no direct bearing on customers or competitors. As researcher Charles Handy at the London Business School concluded:

Trust gives people a sense of belonging. When people feel they're active members of their work community—not merely hired help—they become interested in the company's future and willingly dedicate their time and talent.[119]

Individuals in any department in your company, for example, can benefit from the bonding that comes from working together on challenging problems over extended periods of time. People climb out of warm, safe foxholes, after all, to face bullets because they won't abandon their comrades. It would be hard to imagine a more powerful social force, and equally hard to understand how companies which do not cultivate it can hope to compete.

In the end, character counts, as John Bogle, founder and recently retired chairman of the Vanguard Group entitled a compilation of memos he had written to employees over the years. Trust, as Bogle notes, has to start at the top of the organization. Then at every level, leaders must make it clear that mutual trust is the cardinal corporate virtue. They do this by their actions: honor their own commitments and remove those who do not, no matter how good their numbers.

What Kills It

Recent research shows that the violation of "what's right," *themis* as it was called in ancient Greece, is as damaging in business as in the military where it is a strong risk factor in post traumatic stress disorder.[120] The damage done to individuals by managers' violation of "fair process" in a business is mitigated by the fact that unlike in the military, employees can leave at any time. The best ones, that is, the ones likely to have the most career options, generally are the first to do so.

One effective way to violate "what's right," and so eliminate trust from any organization is for top executives to pay themselves and their immediate coterie multimillion dollar bonuses and guarantee their pension plans, while the company records losses in the hundreds of millions and lays off workers by the thousands. This situation seems to be endemic in the airline industry of the early 21st century, and several have even had the temerity to ask Congress—that is, the American people—to help them foot the bill. Under these circumstances, you can't blame the unions for wanting their piece, too.

Another less egregious but more common way to destroy trust is to succumb to the temptation to control everything. Boyd called this an "obsession for control," and assigns it much of the blame for the bloodbaths that occurred from the mid-1800s to the end of WW I. Most people realize that over-control is the opposite of trust. Yet, many managers still practice it in ways that even they may not realize.

Micromanagers

For most of us in white-collar professions, the greatest threat to mutual trust is the micromanager. Have you ever worked for a one of these people? You know the type, hacks up your report without ever bothering to explain why, moves columns around in tables, and rewrites random sentences. Even if this somehow improved the final product, do you feel that he trusts you? Did the experience improve your intuitive competence? After a while, you lose any thought of initiative or pride of workmanship. Why bother, he is going to change it anyway.

It is impossible to overestimate the damage you can do to yourself through over-control. One of the tasks of senior managers is to spot this tendency and retrain or in the worst case remove the micromanager. However, companies need to keep in mind Deming's distinction between common and special causes. If it's only a few who have a problem with over-control, senior managers should work with them individually. If it's more widespread—much above 10%—then you have a systemic problem that you can only solve by changes to the organizational climate. This would involve an emphasis on trust in management, starting as always at the top, and actions to reward managers who establish and use high trust environments and to remove those who don't, no matter how good their current numbers.

Many companies talk trust, but when sales or profitability begin to shrink, "pull the controls upstairs." That is, they manage by directive, rather than mission, and require that more and more decisions be made at corporate headquarters. Although this may please the bean counters, it slows down OODA loops and hobbles initiative exactly when it is needed most.

Management Style

In fact, the whole notion that we can "control" other human beings is a fallacy. Psychologist Michael Popkin, founder of the highly successful "Active Parenting" program, calls it the "Paradox of Control: The more you try to control a teen, the less you can influence that teen." The reason? "Control eventually leads to resistance, and resistance to rebellion."[121] This is true of all human beings, not only teenagers. One of Boyd's favorite expressions was "The more you try to control people, the less control you get."

Think about it. If explicit control worked, then Eastern Europe would not have thrown off communism, and the Soviet Union, which had controls the likes of which autocratic Western managers could only dream, would have survived and we would all be reading *Secrets of Soviet Management.*

Perks

Although over-control may be the primary killer of mutual trust, there are others. Look at your perk structure. Perks attack mutual trust because their purpose is to discriminate "us" from "them," to create an industrial caste system. So if you have perks, odds are that some fall into the category Tom Peters calls "demeanors." Do reserved parking places contribute to trust? Does an executive dining room? You may have other practices that, while technically not perks, have the same effect. If anybody punches a time clock, does everybody? Do you? Does an executive no-layoff policy that protects senior managers, while shoving workers out the door, build mutual trust, even though it may improve this year's bottom line?

Other Ways to Destroy Mutual Trust

Trust is now recognized as a topic worthy of academic effort. In a recent article in the *Harvard Business Review*, researchers Robert Galford and Anne Siebold Drapeau identified five simple ways to destroy trust in any organization:[122]

1. Inconsistent messages—management proclaims one thing, actually does another
2. Inconsistent standards—people feel that they are being treated differently because of where they work, which legacy organization they came from, etc.
3. Misplaced benevolence—ignoring a poor performing or untrustworthy manager, or employee
4. "Elephants in the parlor"—ignoring the role that office politics actually plays in their organization
5. "Rumors in a vacuum"—senior managers embargo all information, or greatly restrict its flow—i.e., to only certain levels of management—during complex initiatives, merger discussions, restructuring, etc.

Repairing lost trust is difficult, as we all know. Galford and Drapeau recommend redoubling efforts to ensure senior managers are truthful with employees, admit when they don't have or cannot provide critical information, and religiously honor their commitments to provide the information when it is possible to do so. This is all good advice, assuming that you follow through and promote those who practice it and remove those who don't.

Many companies are even farther down on the ladder of trust: they don't destroy it so much as they don't see the need for it in the first place. This attitude is easy to spot, regardless of the fine words in the company vision statement. It took about five minutes, for example, at a company where I once worked, during an orientation for new employees. The very first words out of the HR staffer's mouth (orientation wasn't considered important enough to be conducted by managers) was, "It is a fireable offence for two employees to discuss salaries."

This was a defense contractor, and several of us in the room were former military, where you can look at people and tell within $1,000 per year how much they make. So the obvious question on our minds, as several of us discussed later, was, "What are they trying to hide? What game are they trying to play?" There was no reason trying to build trust in this company, or in helping it improve its performance, since they didn't value trust in the first place. Companies in industries more competitive than defense contracting do not have this luxury.

Finally, there is the management ranking system many companies use. This was a special target of Deming's, since by making recognition a scare resource—there is only one number 1—we set the conditions for Boydian conflict among our own managers. In other words, we do to ourselves what our competitors are struggling to inflict upon us.

Exploit Intuitive Knowledge

Just as mutual trust speeds decision cycles—OODA loops—by groups, especially in times of crisis, intuitive knowledge or "feel," what the Germans called *Fingerspitzengefühl*, allows faster cycles by individuals. With only explicit, provable techniques, it is difficult to discern the patterns in the events that crowd our calendars. This is "right side of the brain" work, and apparently involves mental processing performed by parts of the brain, including the cerebellum, not normally involved in conscious analytical thought.[123]

There is some evidence to indicate that intuitive knowledge is simply the process of "programming" these parts of the brain to give you rapid insights into what would otherwise appear as fragmented, chaotic events. The end result is to become so good at your profession that it really does seem magical, which, of course, is what real magic is all about.

Research has established the validity of intuitive knowledge as propounded by Boyd and the Zen masters. Studies by Gary Klein and his company demonstrated that firefighters and other people who must act quickly in rapidly changing situations with imperfect information do best when their intuition immediately gives them an acceptable course of action. This intuition, of course, is the product of years of experience. Junior military officers beginning their careers were able to make "recognition-primed" decisions (intuition and constructing simple mental models) slightly over 40% of the time. Senior battlefield commanders, on the other hand, were able to rely on recognition-primed faculties in upwards of 95% of their decisions. Formal decision making, of the type typically taught in business schools, is required only when experience is inadequate.[124] Intuitive knowledge is so important in shaping the real world that Klein labeled it as one of the primary "sources of power."

If we look again at the simplified version of the OODA loop from chapter III (reproduced below), we can see how it relies on the speed and power of the implicit, intuitive elements:

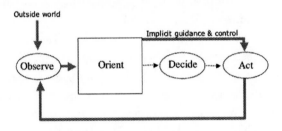

Boyd used the term "implicit guidance and control" similarly to Klein's "recognition primed decisions," that is, in contrast to a formal decision-making methodology that creates and selects among alternatives. Action flows smoothly from orientation. Boyd insisted that we should

> . . . *emphasize implicit over explicit in order to gain a favorable mismatch in friction and time (i.e., ours lower than any adversary) for superiority in shaping and adapting to circumstances.*[125]

The trick is to expand our envelope of intuitive capabilities so that the vast majority of the time, we don't need to utilize a slower explicit decision process. The focus of our effort lies in moving the percentage of time that we can use intuitive knowledge and quick mental simulations to as close to 100% as possible.

This level of skill can be deceiving when seen by others (again, think of a stage magician), because people who have it often don't look like they're working harder or doing things faster. They just, as Musashi insisted, get to a useful result sooner.[126] This is the whole idea behind the Toyota Production System: Create a system where activities become unnecessary—Toyota has a well-defined framework consisting of categories like *muri, mura,* and *muda*[127]—and the whole system operates more quickly, even though the people within it don't appear to be working harder than their competitors anywhere else. This is taught in even the most elementary primer on the system. However, what is sometimes overlooked is that the system works only because of the intuitive competence that Toyota employees develop in sensing these elements and making improvements. If a just-in-time production line had to wait for a formal decision process to work, it would hardly move at all, and it would never improve.

Certainly it takes work and discipline, but once it gets going, superb, intuitive competence also produces extremely high morale, which in turn, reinforces mutual trust and (you guessed it) allows faster OODA loops. Because the Toyota Production System, for example, is so, well, "lean," there is no buffer inventory to cushion against unforeseen interruptions. This means that fast OODA loops are a prerequisite to operating the Toyota Production System as well as one of its outcomes.

When problems do occur the people on the spot are expected to use their skill and initiative to solve them, or, if that is not possible, to summon assistance from the nearest available managers and engineers, and to make this decision quickly and intuitively. It is said that someone who understands the system can walk into a factory, close his or her eyes, and tell by listening and feel if everything is working properly. This ability to sense the state of the system is critical in avoiding major breakdowns and while it may seem magical to an outsider, it develops naturally through increasingly complex interactions with the system.

Where It Comes From

Of course it comes from incessant practice, but practice of a certain type. Because we cannot predict the future in a competitive situation, becoming unusually good at a fixed set of rote activities will not produce victory. Now it is true that as a precondition to intuitive knowledge, the aspiring warrior or executive must practice basic skills so well that they become second nature. In Japanese samurai fencing, *kendo*, the student practices day and night until "sword becomes no-sword; intention becomes no-intention."[128] This is what we mean by tactical skill.

Now you are ready to begin acquiring a true intuitive competence. How? By using these skills in ever more complex circumstances so that you build an intuitive feel for situations where there is a lot of stress and the answers are not clear. We do this through incessant practice, incorporating exposure to an ever-widening variety of new and challenging types of situations, and with feedback from knowledgeable individuals (otherwise we're practicing our mistakes.) We polish individual techniques and also train as a group, thereby building the type of cohesion—mutual trust—that facilitates implicit communication.

As Musashi summarized it, in the translation by Hanshi Steve Kaufman, which was Boyd's favorite:

> *Practice is the only way that you will ever come to understand what the Way of the warrior is about . . . Words can only bring you to the foot of the path . . ."*

This is as true in *The Way of Business* as in any other.

In his classic study on the origins of the Blitzkrieg, military historian and Marine Corps officer Bruce Gudmundsson concluded that the key to decentralized execution, where intuition and initiative can flourish, lies in what he called "a self-educating officer corps." Practically all German officers, he observed, "believed that Germany's fate depended directly upon their tactical competence."[129]

Such obsession with competence does not happen by accident: A company's senior leadership must take on the mission to create and reinforce such a "self-educating" culture. Like so many cultural attributes, this is best done first through example and then by promoting the careers of subordinates who practice it. It is depressing, although certainly it explains a lot, that many companies consider this type education as a cost to be minimized rather than as essential investments.

Many corporate development programs seem to be on the right track when they rotate rising young executives through positions of ever-increasing responsibility throughout the enterprise. But what about the rest of the company? They should also be learning a variety of different skills, and that is what the Japanese do through their emphasis on cross-training programs. There is a limited role in this sort of thing for classroom instruction; a feel for the job has to be acquired on the job(s).

For many years, Germany has built *Fingerspitzengefühl* through an extensive apprenticeship program that involves practically everybody from baker to banker. On the blue collar side, the program culminates in the creation of a final sample product, a true "masterpiece."

How to Kill It

Believe it or not, there actually are companies that discourage this type of competence. Deming rails against organizations that don't understand the importance of requiring first-line supervisors to have expertise in the jobs they manage. How can a supervisor have a "feel" for how his operation is going if he's never done it?

Many US companies give little importance to training their blue-collar workers. They think nothing of spending $10,000 to send a senior manager to a 3-week executive seminar, which may well be justifiable, but begrudge the "lost time" hourly workers accrue for even a 1-hour quality improvement class. You can imagine what this does for mutual trust.

Specialist or Strategist?

Isn't it true that the more you practice, the better you get? Yes, but, and this bears repeating, the intuitive mastery we are striving for is not brilliant skill at predictable tasks. As the late science fiction author, Robert Heinlein, pointed out, specialization is for insects. Humans need the mystifying ability to cope with the unpredictable and ambiguous challenges posed by thinking adversaries in the real world.

Since *kendo* masters practice hard, don't we need to put in long hours to develop super competence? The answer is absolutely yes. However, sixteen hours at the office doing the same things day after day simply make you a workaholic (and very likely a micromanager); they do not *per se* confer an intuitive skill useful in competitive situations. Tom Peters suggests that you can spot who is going to do great things by what they do on airplanes. They don't pull out the laptop and grind spreadsheets. Instead, they "read *Zen and the Art of Motorcycle Maintenance* for the umpteenth time," or pick up insights on human behavior from the great novelists.

Implement the Contract of Leadership

It doesn't take much leadership ability to understand why mutual trust and competence are important. The next two aspects of this organizational climate for operational success may be less familiar. Both the concepts of *mission* and *focus* allow a superior to make sure that the intent of his subordinates harmonizes with his own, without stifling the subordinates' initiative and in consequence, without slowing down the organization's OODA loops.

Between individuals, the device the Germans came up with is the mission, which we can consider as a contract, or *Auftrag*, between superior and subordinate. Back in chapter III, on agility, I described how this works in war. In today's chaotic, ruthlessly competitive commercial environment, business needs such a device, and a little experimenting should convince you that *mission* works here as well.

Responsibility

You will rapidly discover that a mutually agreed understanding—a contract of sorts—is a wonderful device for fostering a sense of responsibility among the people at your company. Because they have to consider, think, and agree, rather than acquiesce, you will sense increased morale and improved dedication. All of this, of course, reinforces mutual trust and implicit communication, which, as we have seen, are critical elements in increasing your OODA loop speed.

Perhaps the greatest value of viewing responsibility as a contract is that it provides an alternative to over-control. Micromanaging is simply not allowed: Once he or she accepts the contract, the subordinate has total freedom within the constraints of the contract as to how to proceed. There is no place for the stack of reports that allow managers or headquarters staffers to second guess every decision.

At Nissan and Toyota, project managers for new models enjoy total control over the car's design and engineering. Senior managers, even the president of the corporation, are forbidden from interfering, once they have approved the project. As long ago as 1989, Nissan developed the Maxima in 30 months, roughly half the US industry's average at the time and well below it even today, with such quality that the year it was introduced, it topped the J. D. Power initial quality survey.[130]

Communication

As a complement to the "do or die" nature of Boyd's concept of mission, people communicate in a steady stream back to the boss. With a suitable level of trust and cohesion, these messages can be brief and just report progress or highlight exceptions and problems. This helps upper management maintain an appreciation for the overall progress of the organization. Communications is the bottoms-up aspect of command and control, and the Marines define "control," to be this stream of information:

> *Control takes the form of feedback—the continuous flow of information about the unfolding situation returning to the commander—which allows the commander to adjust and modify command action as needed.*[131]

Smooth upward communications is not as easy as it might seem. Some of the news may be bad, or may reveal mistakes or poor judgment on the part of the person doing the communicating. Still, the boss has to know, if he or she is going to form a true appreciation of the situation, and the sooner the better. Obviously arranging the work environment so that people will report failure or mistakes to persons who can immediately fire them requires a high level of mutual trust, and is yet another example of why trust is *The Way of Management and Leadership*.

Good communication can also protect the subordinate. If, despite your best efforts, your project isn't going too well, perhaps isn't going at all, and may not even be possible, you should take care that this fact comes as no surprise to your boss.

She or he has a number of options, other than simply throwing you out or forcing you to keep beating your head against the wall. Remember, s/he wants the whole organization to succeed and, given some advance warning, can use his or her feel for things to reinforce you, or shift the focus of effort to a more promising direction. Or, let's be realistic, find something else for you to do if you've signed up for more than you can handle. Obviously it takes a lot of mutual trust to know whom to appoint to which missions and especially to admit and quickly communicate mistakes.

This contractual device provides such high levels of motivation that the more drastic options are rarely needed. You will have a tremendous pride in negotiating and accepting the contract, in owning it. There is nothing worse than failing it.

Where It Comes From

The introduction to these concepts, in the chapter on agility, explained that before you can manage via the mission concept, you have to be well on your way to increasing mutual trust and creating intuitive understanding in coping with uncertainty. Once these are underway, then simply begin. The most important thing you can do is to use it yourself, in every action with your people. Then insist that they use it in all actions with the people who work for them.

There is no formula, for the idea is antithetical to strategy, for making a mission-type arrangement. Concentrate instead on the essence of the concept, which is to devolve maximum responsibility onto the subordinate, in return for his or her pledge to use his/her initiative and creativity to accomplish the task, consistent with your ground rules. Here are a few observations to help you get started. You can, at first, be a little more formal than you may find necessary later on. Remind yourself to include a clear statement of the concept that gives your mission focus and direction, which we'll explore in more detail in the next section.

Gary Klein, in his seminal work, *Sources of Power* (another book, which along with his next, *Intuition at Work*, should be in every manager's and strategist's desk drawer), illustrates the intuitive / implicit nature of a business contract (drawing on Karl Weick's version of a conversation between a boss and a team member):

- Here's what I think we face
- Here's what I think we should do, and why
- Here's what we should keep our eye on
- Now, talk to me[132]

The only thing needed to make this into a mission order is to look your subordinate right in the eyes and say,

- Here's what I want you and your team to accomplish. Will you do it?

Bill Lind, who played a key role in introducing maneuver warfare into the Marine Corps, and whom we met in chapter III, suggests that every mission order actually contains an explicit or implied "in order to." In a business setting, this might look like:

> Susan, I need you to go down and take charge of sales in the Northeast and increase revenue by at least 25% in order to avoid factory shut downs that could start as early as July.

In other words, your intent is to avoid a break in production, and the disruption that comes with temporary closing of the factory. Her mission, should she decide to accept it, (sorry) is to ramp up sales to keep the factory going.

She may need to take a few days to assess the situation—why are sales down? Is the product line out of date or too expensive (i.e., are there factors out of her control that would keep her from accomplishing the mission?) Or has the sales program been mismanaged (something she might fix.) Does she need the authority to hire additional sales force?

How much flexibility will she have to negotiate prices and promise delivery schedules?

She should then come back to you and have a frank discussion. Because you know her past performance, you trust that if she accepts, she will deliver, if delivery is in any way possible. You should also negotiate other requirements, such as any need to coordinate with other activities in the organization. You can write any of this down if you need to, and for financial aspects it would be a good idea, but verbal communication is much quicker, and shows a higher level of mutual trust (assuming that it's there), than does a written mission. Of course, as your group works together and builds mutual trust, more and more of this communication will naturally become implicit, with all of the benefits mentioned above.

Do not prescribe how to accomplish the job. The less said about the how, the better. If you don't have a strong belief, grounded in past experience, that Susan can think of ways to accomplish this mission (whether she realizes it yet or not), you should not be assigning it to her: Mutual trust / cohesion / unity yet one more time.

Discuss it for a few minutes (or whatever it takes) to convince yourself that you and Susan both have the same mental concept of what needs to be done. Then give her a little time to think about the matter. A top caliber subordinate can get quite blunt: She may question whether your idea makes sense and whether you have offered her enough time or resources to do the job. This questioning is key to transferring ownership of the job, and your answering these serves the same purpose that answering objections does in any selling job, what salespersons call "closing on objections."

But it's more than just selling. You might also discover that your expectations were too low. Maybe she feels capable of accomplishing more than you first thought, and you must use your judgment to decide if this is a risk worth taking. Or maybe she has noticed something that you missed and really does have a better idea. You may have to do some negotiating to arrive at a contract that both meets your intent and gains her commitment. You can play this role to the hilt: think James Bond and M.

Finally, however, you've got to close. A mission contract is a two-sided personal commitment, eyeball-to-eyeball, and there are only two options: Either she takes the contract or she doesn't. In the military, a legal order must be obeyed, but business is not war and you should probably allow a subordinate to opt out, if he or she remains unconvinced that your idea makes sense or is within his or her capabilities. Incidentally, if this happens very often, it could be a symptom of a serious erosion of mutual trust. However, if in the end your subordinate declines, then you should probably change the terms or find somebody else.

This procedure may seem cumbersome, but it actually reflects the way commanders issue orders in combat. The thing that makes it a contract is the negotiation process, which gains commitment by the subordinate, and usually pumps up her enthusiasm as well. Once the process becomes embedded in your culture, and if you really have a high degree of trust, much of the negotiation will be quick and implicit—you've worked together long enough to detect when somebody has lingering doubts, loyally suppressed.

How to Kill It

Micromanage, or by any other action fail to live up to your end of the contract.

Provide Focus and Direction

By using a contractual arrangement you can harmonize the intent of a superior and subordinate, and still encourage your people to take the initiative. This is fine for a specific task, but you will also need a device for harmonizing the actions of large groups, and ultimately, everybody in your organization, while also encouraging initiative. In chapter III, we saw how the Germans used the concept of focus (*Schwerpunkt*) for this purpose. Once the focus was designated, subordinates could use their own initiatives and make rapid decisions so that their actions support the main effort. Of course, top leaders could shift the focus of effort to exploit opportunities created during the operation. In a sense, a focus identifies the "What is to be done" and the mission contract empowers people to do it.

What we are trying to do is align, through positive and encouraging means, everybody's efforts in a company. As Tom Wolfe wrote of Robert Noyce, one of the founders of both Fairchild Semiconductor and Intel:

> *Noyce wanted them to all keep internalizing the company's goals and to provide their own motivations, just as they had during the start-up phase. If they did that, they would have the capacity to make their own decisions.*[133]

You will find that by employing the *Schwerpunkt* concept, you can achieve Noyce's purpose, and because people can see that what they're doing is contributing to the overall objective, an actionable focus does wonders for morale. The head of IBM, Sam Palmisano, appears to be taking this approach. IBM under Lou Gerstner, who famously said that the last thing IBM needed was a "vision," morphed from a vendor of mainframes to a company that derives the bulk of its profit from services and consulting advice. Despite his cynicism, Gerstner's concept did provide clear and actionable direction for the time. It also put IBM in competition with pure consulting companies, like EDS, CSC, and an alphabet soup of competitors.

So Palmisano is trying a new focus: "IBM would supply computing power as if it were water or electricity."[134] Computing power on demand. This concept has the potential to provide focus and direction—be an actionable vision—if Palmisano flows it down through the IBM organization, and managers at each level absorb it and set actionable focuses for their teams that guide people throughout their daily activities in harmony with it: When in doubt, move in the direction that facilitates computing on demand.

It would be nice if a company's highest-level focus also served the purposes of grand strategy (attract the uncommitted to our side, while pumping up our morale and deflating that of the competition) noted in chapter IV. The best way, though, for a commercial enterprise to do this is to provide products and services that people want to buy, and leave saving humanity to the non-profits. Honda's headband slogan during the H-Y War (described in chapter I) was the decidedly uncouth "*Yamaha wo tsubusu!*" a "rather impolite" expression roughly meaning "We will crush, squash, butcher, slaughter, etc. Yamaha!"[135] One may assume the phrase made no appeal to the good of all mankind, but it did its job.

Most of us are more like Honda than like the Little Sisters of Charity, and taking pride in the quality of our work, enjoying the company of our compatriots, and driving our competition into Chapter 11 will have to suffice.

Goals

Perhaps the most common device for giving people focus and direction is goal setting, but goals, as often as they are used, have their pros and cons. Sure, if you can convince everybody that profits must increase 20% next quarter or we're going out of business, people will hurry around looking for ways to hype profits by 20%. When discussing "mission" I assigned Susan a goal of 25% improvement in sales, based on what I calculated was needed to avoid closing the factory and on what I felt her district could reasonably provide. It was not a number pulled from the ether, and I went to some length to explain this to her. Short of any such basis in reality, people will often do the easiest things, such as firing 20% of the workforce, canceling vital R&D programs, or simply not making any payments to suppliers. In other words, they will take achieving the goal as seriously as they feel you were in setting it; they will sense whether you have positioned yourself at the *Schwerpunkt.*

Goals, as we all know, can be motivators. Cypress Semiconductor, a communications-oriented company founded in 1982, used to have a computer that tracked the thousands of self-imposed goals that its people fed into the system. Cypress founder T. J. Rodgers identified this automated goal tending system as the heart of his management style and a big factor in the company's early success.[136]

Frankly, I find this philosophy depressing, not to mention a temptation to focus inward: If the boss places great importance on entering and tracking goals, as he obviously does, then that is what the other employees are going to consider important.[137] In any case, what's the big deal about meeting or missing a goal? A goal is an intention at a point in time. It is, to a large extent, an arbitrary target, whether you set it or someone above you assigns it. And we all know that numerical goals can be gamed, like banking (delaying) sales that we could have made this quarter to help us make quota next quarter. Unlike a *Schwerpunkt*, which gives focus and direction for chaotic and uncertain situations, what does a goal tell you? Just keep your head down and continue plugging away?

Rod Canion, founder of Compaq Computer Corporation, must have agreed, "We set directions rather than goals."[138] He points out that a reasonable goal for Compaq's first year revenues (1983) might have been as high as $50 million. However, if they had hit that goal in the third quarter, everybody would have been tempted to coast the rest of the year. Instead, they kept concentrating on things like quality, technology, and rapid development cycles, and finished the year with revenues of $111 million—a record at the time for a start-up's first year. What would have been a reasonable goal for 1989? Five hundred million? Actually Compaq did a totally unpredictable $3 billion that year.

Futurist James Ogilvy simply denounced managing through goal setting as "bunk." Instead, he recommends that:

> *Organizations should tread near the edge of the future, making it up as they go along, with as much sensitivity, awareness, knowledge, compassion, feeling, and beauty as they can muster.*[139]

The point is that although goals are one way to focus people's efforts, they should be used sparingly. As Canion complains, they answer the question, "What does 'good enough' mean?" In a sense, they are the antithesis of a true focusing device, since they provide no guidance about what to do once you've reached your goal. In Susan's example, what if she makes the 25% improvement goal in 9 months—does she and her sales team take the rest of the year off?

If you are going to use goals anyway, never impose them on someone else or on yourself without explaining where they came from and why they're important. Any mission should include a statement of the commander's intent ("in order to" or equivalent) and information on missions two levels up. Same is true should you decide to assign a goal. "Cut costs by 15%!" you say. Why 15%? Why not 20%? If we can cut costs by 15% now, why haven't we already done it? Is management accusing us of being shiftless, wasteful, and lazy to the tune of 15%?

Maybe they don't know what to do to control costs, so they are simply going to order them down.

Returning to our example of Susan and the 25% goal in order to save the factory, if the immediate circumstances were different, I might frame the mission differently:

> *Sales in the Northeast have been falling the last three quarters. Our top two competitors are gaining market share at our expense. From my experience, and from what I'm seeing in other regions, it isn't the fault of the product. I want you to go down there, get this turned around, and put our sales effort back on track in order to ensure a growth rate that the board will find acceptable, if not impressive.*

Notice that I didn't say by how much to improve sales. The more the better, but in this example, her focus is "getting the sales effort back on track," which implies that I know what a well-oiled sales machine feels like, regardless of a specific month's numbers.

This example drives home an important point: There is no substitute for knowing what you're doing. In business, numbers bounce up and down all the time. It takes real management skill, *Fingerspitzengefühl*, to disregard the daily turbulence and sense that you're on the right track (as in the Nelson Funnel metaphor at the end of the last chapter), or to feel uneasy about an organization, even though its numbers look great, today:

> *Sales of our last two products met the head office's estimates, but somehow our new stuff didn't have the flair that I want in our products. When I'm out talking to customers, nobody complains, but nobody's raving about us, either. I'm concerned that our product development effort has become too bureaucratic, and we're setting ourselves up to get ambushed by a competitor sometime soon. I want you to take charge of product development and get us back on track, pronto. I also want your recommendations about what I and the rest of senior management can do to support this effort—which I regard as the most important undertaking for the company right now.*

Another example:

Our financial reporting system isn't supporting our manufacturing and R&D efforts the way I think it should. We regard R&D as a profit center, which is forcing them to make decisions that I think are short-sighted. Sure, it's keeping Wall Street happy, for now, but I believe we've created a system that encourages us to eat our seed corn. We can't blame R&D management, though, for getting the most out of the incentive program that we set up. You used to run R&D, and you've had a lot of experience in finance, so I want you to take over as EVP of Finance and create a system that works in harmony with our overall objective of leading the world in new product innovation.

In any company, our notion of focus and direction should include the idea of continually studying and improving company systems. You will notice that this is implicit in the three examples above. I did not tell them what "good enough" was. If pressed, I'd probably say something like "Better than the current best and improving—strengthening our climate, eliminating unnecessary functions, simplifying, reducing waste, polishing our quality, and reducing cycle times that affect customers . . ." They would just know.

An Alternative to Goals

A reporter once asked an official from Toyota whether the company achieved "six sigma" quality—a defect rate of around 3 in a million and also the name of a quality improvement methodology that is currently fashionable. His answer typifies the Boyd approach to goals:

Basically, I would say that because of our evolutionary concept, whatever we were doing becomes the benchmark for what we do next. We hold onto what we were doing so that it becomes maintainable and it is the new steady state.[140]

This may seem like a masterwork of obfuscation, but it is entirely consistent with Toyota's overall guiding concept:

> *The Toyota Production System, quite simply, is about shortening the time it takes to convert customer orders into vehicle deliveries.*[141]

This is one of the best vision / focusing statements in the world of business. Instead of setting arbitrary goals, it tells everybody who works for Toyota that whenever they are in doubt about what to do, take the action that will reduce customer-to-delivery span time. It sets a direction, not a goal, since wherever we are this year, we will be better next year.

Wouldn't this lead to poor quality, as workers rush to compress manufacturing time? No, and to see why, you need to analyze Toyota's statement carefully (ever notice how everybody in Japan seems to write in the style of Sun Tzu?) Toyota did not say that they want to shorten the time taken to perform each activity within the system. This is worth repeating: the purpose of the TPS is to shorten overall order-to-delivery time. It does not follow that the best way to do this is to try to compress the time taken by each activity within it.

That way would not work and would indeed lead to poor quality. It is more likely that they would shorten the delivery span by finding ways to eliminate activities, since an activity eliminated takes no time to perform (it also adds no defects and costs nothing.) Similarly, they don't try to rush decisions, like what type of water pump the car will have. In fact, there is a concept within both Toyota's development and production systems known as "learning how to wait," based on the notion that it takes less time to do something right than to do it over. Thus they would not be interested in making decisions earlier on the factory floor. They would rather make the decision at the appropriate time, and put more thought (more OODA loop cycles) into it.

The subtitle of one of the few papers on the Toyota Development System reinforces this bias: "How delaying decisions can make better cars faster."[142] This is entirely consistent with the *Schwerpunkt* concept, where all activities must support the focus of effort, even if this means not (sub-) optimizing their own performance.

As Boyd noted:

> Schwerpunkt *represents a unifying medium that provides a directed way to tie initiative of many subordinate actions with superior intent*

as a basis to diminish friction and compress time in order to generate a
favorable mismatch in time/ability to shape and adapt to unfolding
circumstances.[143]

Through their years of training and working together, the members of a well-functioning Toyota Production System facility have learned how to flow down the top level focus to the individual cells and other elements of the system in a way much more sophisticated than simply optimizing the performance of each. It is these specific techniques— with the weird names characteristic of the TPS: *takt* time, *kanban*, *jidoka*, *heijunka*, and so on—that people learn when they study the system.

Flowdown

Now let's look at harmonizing focus at different levels within the organization. In general, the same principles apply. In the military, a commander would assign missions to subordinates, with objectives for them to achieve regarding the enemy. The commander would ensure that they understood his/her intent and those of commanders two levels up. In business, you might also use specific objectives, but, as noted above, there is often a competitive advantage to be gained from giving people that you can trust broad areas, setting directions in other words, and turning them loose.

If I am a manager at some level, running a sensor group, for example, I have a direction (or objective or other information) from my boss, which then forms part of my strategy. I have a feel for where sensor technology is going. I may also have a specific set of products I am developing sensors for, and for these I will need to take milestones into account. Considering all this, I use my judgment, experience, guile, whatever, to create a focusing concept for my organization:

First, our performance is state of the art and progressing nicely. Customers
I talk to are all excited about how our stuff works. But we are about 5%

too expensive compared to our competitors and our best products still use about 10% more power than where I think we need to be. So I want to concentrate our efforts in these two areas and be ready to support the launch of our new series in May.

What I've done is told everybody what I consider important and in which direction they should make their trade-offs. Based on this, I can give direction / focus to the teams within my group to ensure that they are working on problems that will further my (and the company's) overall efforts, without constraining their initiative in solving these problems. In addition, since they know the focus several levels up, they can be on the lookout for new techniques and technologies that while not specifically within their area, could help the company elsewhere.

At any given time, if I have done my job right, my whole organization will function according to its *Schwerpunkt* (the one I derived from my mission / direction) by the fact that my people are operating according to theirs. As with our discussion of mission, I cannot give you a formula for flowing focus and direction to sub-groups and teams nor, as Musashi insists many times, will you master the concept by reading a book (this or any other). You must try these concepts, practice them, create mechanisms for sharing experiences, develop common outlooks and orientations, and manage by them. Armed with the general idea and a willingness to experiment (and make mistakes), you can develop the skills with this concept that have served successful leaders so well in the past.

Can You Have More Than One?

Focus and direction mean more than "major effort." Can you have more than one focus of effort? In the military, most authors on maneuver warfare agree that you cannot. In fact, in the Marine Corps, the commander designates one unit and its mission as the *Schwerpunkt*. As we have seen, all of the other units in that command must support the *Schwerpunkt*.

In business, the situation is not so clear, since a focus will generally be a concept rather than a business unit. A concept such as Toyota's "constantly reduce customer order to delivery time" clearly provides focus and can cover a wide variety of product lines. The question of multiple focuses in business is probably an area where it is best not to become dogmatic: If there is no guiding focus for the organization as a whole, then drop down to the business units. *"Yamaha wo tsubusu!"* worked great for Honda motorcycles, and for 18 months. Other units of Honda at the time needed other concepts to give them focus and guide initiative.

If there is no guiding concept for the whole operation, it becomes the job of top management to ensure that the focuses of the individual elements do not conflict. If this proves impossible, then management should divest or realign, based on the idea that the ultimate foundation for competitiveness is mutual trust, which is impossible to achieve in a company where units work at cross purposes. They should take this action even if the accountants advise that it will hurt short-term profits.

Schwerpunkt: Summary

However you define the *Schwerpunkt* for your organization, here are some ideas for you to consider:

- It has to actually provide focus and direction. It has to give real and *actionable guidance* in situations where there is no formal direction. This is what distinguishes a *Schwerpunkt* from a "vision statement."
- It must contribute to an outward focus, towards the customer and the marketplace. The last thing you need is another device that drives your attention inward, which is the problem with so many "goals." Always keep in mind: "We will crush, squash, butcher, slaughter, etc. Yamaha!" and "The length of time between when a *customer* orders a Toyota and when s/he receives it."
- Your focus should reinforce mutual trust. You must make sure that it flows down to every member of your organization. This makes it a powerful tool of "control" in the best sense of helping

people make the right decisions, in turbulent times, without destroying their initiatives.

- Finally, people in every organization at every level within the company must understand the concept and use it to run their affairs. As I've said so many times, the key is: study it, believe it, and then promote those who use it and remove those who do not, and this starts at the top.

How to Get It

It's not a question of "getting it," it's a matter of doing it. Setting the focus and direction and shifting it in response to the circumstances are functions of leaders (note that I did not write "managers") at every level of the company. Look over some of your planning documents and communications with employees: do you see anything that will focus people's efforts and encourage them to take the initiative? When you are talking to people about what needs to be done, will they perceive a concept so simple and strong that it will motivate them and guide everything they do?

How to Kill It

The *Schwerpunkt* concept offers a powerful management tool, but only if you employ it to shape the marketplace. Because the future is the future—uncertain, ambiguous, and at least partially under the control of others who do not wish you well—you will sometimes have to shift your focus, and there cannot be a formula for this process. We wouldn't need executives otherwise. To make the idea work, you will need a strongly developed intuitive competence for making these types of decisions. A good way to kill it, therefore, is simply not to use it, which guarantees that you will not develop the skill to use it. Whether this happens through incompetence, or fear, or, as in the case of Hitler against Russia, through arrogance really does not make much difference.

A Graphical Representation

Perhaps Boyd's climate is easiest to visualize if we start with the individual and work up (Boyd always did prefer the bottom-up approach.) Individuals cultivate and polish their intuitive competence, *Fingerspitzengefühl*, for the jobs they hold—whether lathe operator, junior drafter, engineer, sales person, project leader, or senior executive. Represent this by small rectangles (bear with me.)

Figure 13—Individual Competence

Einheit is usually translated as "unity" or "mutual trust." But as Boyd noted, it can also be thought of as a super-*Fingerspitzengefühl*— it suggests the competence of the group, working together to accomplish some purpose. So *Einheit* aligns the rectangles, although not rigidly.

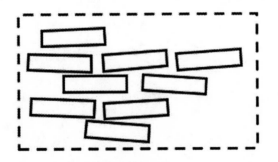

Figure 14—*Einheit* Represents Intuitive Competence of
the Group

Schwerpunkt provides focus and direction to aim the entire organization towards that goal or purpose.

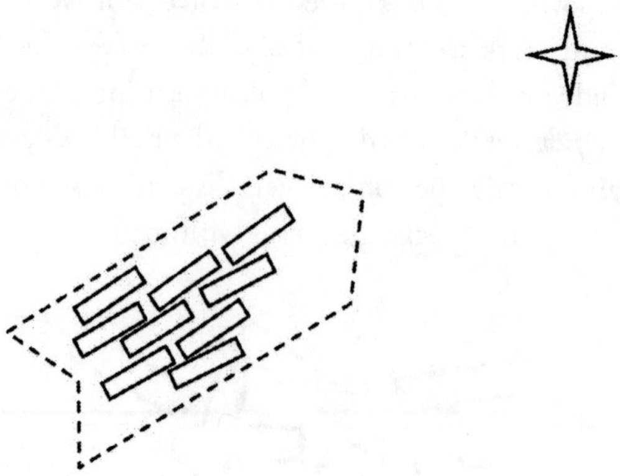

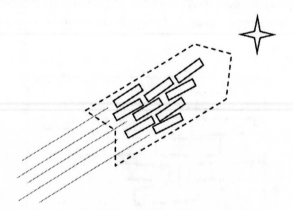

Figure 15—*Schwerpunkt* Aims the Organization

And finally, the mission contract, *Auftrag,* provides the energy, the motive force to encourage the members of the group towards accomplishment of the common goal.

Figure 16—*Auftrag* Provides the Power

Pulling It All Together

Boyd's metaphor of strategy as a mental tapestry, rather than a chart or map, suggests that at the level of individuals and small units, the action may seem confused and complex, but that when viewed in its whole, a pattern must emerge to accomplish a higher purpose. One mechanism for achieving this harmony is known as *Einsickern* in German, "reconnaissance pull" in maneuver warfare, and through analogy by phrases like "exploratory marketing" in business texts.[144] The basic idea is to start a number of things going and reinforce the ones that succeed. This seems reasonable, but a closer look at its strategic roots suggests that it is not enough.

In maneuver warfare, which Boyd's work helped establish in the US military, commanders do not just dump a bunch of units on the battlefield and watch to see if any start to succeed. Instead, maneuver warfare units need a more active mechanism to force opportunities, a device robust enough to endure the stress and confusion of combat, yet one that allows subordinates to seize fleeting opportunities, all the while accomplishing the overall objectives assigned to the operation.

One device used by maneuver warfare, as we have seen, for creating and exploiting the chaos created by multiple initiatives is focus and direction, the *Schwerpunkt*. The actions of all the other units, that is, the *Nebenpunkte,* or "secondary points," support the focus.[145] At the start of the operation the commander will often make an explicit designation of the *Schwerpunkt,* but with the right culture, most of the shifting of it during the heat of battle will occur implicitly as the action progresses. It's not so much the fact of having a *Schwerpunkt* that makes maneuver warfare powerful, but the way the members of the unit can shift the focus to confuse the enemy and create and exploit weaknesses.

Typically in maneuver warfare, a commander will set out an aggressive reconnaissance, a strong force in front of the main body that probes and tests the enemy. When it finds or creates a gap, the units that are not in the reserve (which belongs to the commander and awaits his orders) will sense the new situation and begin to exploit in accordance with the commander's intent. The *Schwerpunkt* has shifted, but in an implicit and organic way. The current situation is pulling the units to a critical area, analogous to how customers pull product through a company operating under lean production.

The important point is that maneuver warfare is high tempo

warfare. People don't wait around for the commander to make a "decision" before taking action, although the best commanders somehow seem to be at the *Schwerpunkt* when things start to break loose. With enough mutual experience and trust—*Einheit*—people throughout the organization know what to do and will take the initiative to make it happen.

Quickness is critical, because a gap will only be an opportunity for a brief period, until the enemy force reorients. If the enemy's collective OODA loop is quicker than ours (reflecting their *Einheit* and *Fingerspitzengefühl*), they could arrange traps or ambushes of our penetrating forces. If ours is quicker, we can create or find gaps and exploit them faster than the enemy can cope and perhaps precipitate a collapse and rout.[146]

The same implicit, organic quickness and initiative also powers successful businesses. Note that I am **not** saying that the specific tactics of maneuver warfare—or any other form of warfare—apply to business. However I am claiming that Boyd's underlying strategy—the use of time as a shaping and exploiting mechanism, and the emphasis on a culture / organizational climate that makes this possible—apply equally well to both.

As an example of how this could work in business, visualize a well-oiled sales team trying to close a big project. If a member senses from prospects' reactions that the original focus on cost isn't going to close the sale, but there is an interest in quick delivery times, the focus will shift to the new direction. On great sales teams, any member can ask a closing question if he or she detects that the buying moment has arrived, and the other members will transition smoothly into their supporting roles.

Sometimes, though, the only way to shift the focus is to tell the organization outright, hence, an *explicit* decision that you communicate unambiguously to your team. You might find this technique most useful for large organizations that need a dramatic change in direction, such as IBM under Gerstner and then Palmisano. Intel also used an explicit shift of focus to implement top management's decision to convert from memory chips, which were rapidly becoming a commodity, to the more complex but higher margin microprocessors. Although this action appeared logical to senior executives in Intel, they realized that it might not seem compelling to people who had devoted their careers to developing, manufacturing, and selling memory chips. So they launched a campaign and worked hard to sell the new direction throughout the organization—it became the *Schwerpunkt* for top management at Intel for a couple of years.[147] Now, hardly anybody remembers that Intel ever made memory chips.

Senior management must also assure that their personnel policies align with the new focus, so that people advance in the organization as they progress in the new direction. Unfortunately, there will be some small percentage who will not head down the new path. They must be removed, after an amount of effort and a period of time that the members of the organization consider reasonable. *Themis*, "what's right," must always be preserved.

Implementing Boyd's Organizational Climate

Organizations that create a climate such as that described in this chapter will naturally experience an acceleration of their OODA loops. So the question becomes how to install it. Boyd suggested, in his briefing "Organic Design for Command and Control," that it will grow naturally if the senior management sets the proper conditions. He defines the two essential elements necessary for running any human organization along maneuver conflict—rapid OODA loop—lines as:

- **Leadership**—implies the art of inspiring people to enthusiastically take action towards **uncommon** goals. It must interact with the system to shape the character or nature of that system in order to realize what is to be done.
- **Appreciation**—refers to the recognition of worth or value, clear perception, understanding, comprehension, discernment, etc. It must **not** interact nor interfere with the system, but must discern (not shape) the character / nature of what is being done or about to be done.

Without mutual trust, you will not be able to interpret the implicit signals your team members are sending you as you exercise appreciation. Chuck Spinney, a close colleague of Boyd's, tells of sitting in on an interview Boyd conducted in the early 1980s with two German generals, Hermann Balck, whom the Germans regarded as one of their top field commanders, and his chief of staff, F. W. von Mellenthin. Boyd set out a simple scenario and then asked Balck to show him how he and von Mellenthin worked together in the field. Balck asked von Mellenthin for his assessment and then sat with an intent but perfectly blank expression while von Mellenthin play-acted a response.

Balck immediately made his decision, whereupon he became expressive and highly animated. Suddenly he was back at the front and trying to convey quickly and completely what he wanted done. Spinney concluded that during the appreciation phase, Balck was closely observing von Mellenthin, but was also careful not to influence von Mellenthin by even the smallest gesture. During the leadership phase, he was trying to ensure that he did influence von Mellenthin as strongly and as quickly as possible, using a mixture of verbal and physical cues that von Mellenthin had learned to interpret, and leaving quite a bit unspoken.

If you read the definition of "appreciation" carefully, you might conclude that you will have to develop mechanisms for sensing the health and progress of the organization outside the formal reporting lines. This is true, you will. Andy Grove at Intel, for example, spent a couple of hours every day reading e-mail. It also probably wouldn't hurt to get out of our office and talk to people once in a while. The main idea of appreciation is to learn what's really going on in your organization without causing the organization to react to your observing. Otherwise your observation is meaningless, because the organization will have changed in response to it. Again, mutual trust is paramount, because without it you will be seen as micromanaging, spying on your employees, and circumventing the ability of middle managers to do their jobs.[148]

Orientation, as Boyd insisted in all his briefings, is what guides and shapes the OODA loop. "Orientation is the *Schwerpunkt*," he insists, shaping the way we interact with the environment.[149] "Installing" the culture means "shaping the character or nature" of the company, which means the same thing as changing the orientation of not only the organization but of the people in it. The idea is that installation (or "culture change" as it was once called) will proceed naturally once leaders create the right conditions.

You can think of it as a four-element, never-ending process, where the steps start at the top (perhaps with coaxing and preaching from subordinates) but then proceed down and continue simultaneously throughout the organization:

- Study it, as you are doing now. Read everything you can. Talk to others who have tried it, whether successfully or not.
- Make implementing this culture the *Schwerpunkt*. This means that all the other activities of the company must support implementation. Personnel policies, outsourcing decisions, accounting methods—all activities must be evaluated not only on their own merits, but also on how they affect unity, cohesion, trust, mission concepts, intuitive competence, and so forth. At first, questions like these must be agenda items at virtually every meeting. As you become proficient, consideration of the impact on culture will become implicit.
- Promote those who study, embrace, and use it.
- Remove those who do not, no matter how good their numbers.

Unfortunately, you should expect to remove about 25-40% of your current management, some because they will not participate in adopting the new climate (they must leave the company) but most of them because once the new system is in place, the functions they were performing will no longer be necessary. As the late Admiral Hyman Rickover, father of the nuclear Navy, once observed, in any organization there are doers and checkers—you will find that in the new organization you will need a lot fewer checkers, but if you leave them in place, they will start checking again.

You must play fair with this last group, however, in order to build the trust and cohesion you will need among the survivors. It's the right thing to do, even if it costs you some short-term profit. You must preserve *themis*. After all, they became middle managers by excelling in the system the way it was at the time. If you cannot find places elsewhere in the company where they can contribute in the new system, you must offer severance packages that they and the survivors will view as fair, that is, within the envelope of "what's right." As Machiavelli noted in *The Prince*, the best practice is to carry out this procedure in one "Night of Long Knives," and then immediately swing to the rebuilding mode.

Through leadership and appreciation at all levels you continue to improve the climate, weeding out naysayers, promoting the doers, and everybody studies, experiments, and shares their knowledge and experiences. General Electric, America's most profitable company in 2002, has an institution, the John F. Welch Leadership Center, known as "Crotonville," at Ossing, New York, to accelerate that change. As the company notes on its Web site:

> *It began to take its present form in 1982 when newly appointed Chairman John. F. Welch saw that the dramatic changes in culture and thinking he envisioned for GE would require a company-wide initiative. He saw Crotonville as the tool to implement and spread that change throughout GE.*

Similarly, the military services have an extensive collection of training centers, schools, and colleges, some of which are accredited, degree-granting institutions, to ensure that their culture and doctrine promulgate throughout the organization. You need a similar mechanism both to teach the new culture and to demonstrate that you consider it important. For a small company or team, it can be something as simple as gathering everybody together once a week for an hour to discuss and brainstorm these ideas.

Place yourself at the *Schwerpunkt* of cultural change: the people who work for you will take it as seriously as you do, which is what leadership is all about.

How Long Will It Take?

You can't blame people for wanting instant results. Time is money, and quickness, especially quick OODA loops, is good. But when it comes to adopting maneuver conflict / Boyd's principles to your business, there is a lot to be learned and a lot to be done. Consider that:

- According to its principle creator, Taiichi Ohno, it took 28 years (1945-1973) to create and install the Toyota Production System, which is maneuver conflict applied to manufacturing.
- It takes roughly 15 years of experience—and recognition as a leader in one's technical field—to qualify as a *susha* (development manager) for a new Toyota vehicle.[150]
- Studies of people regarded as the top experts in a number of fields suggest that they practice about four hours a day, virtually every day, for 10 years before they achieve a recognized level of mastery.[151]
- It takes a minimum of 8 years beyond a bachelor's degree to train a surgeon (4 years medical school and 4 or more years of residency.)
- It takes four to six years on the average beyond a bachelor's degree to complete a Ph.D.
- It takes three years or so to earn a black belt (first degree) in the martial arts and four to six years beyond that to earn third degree, assuming you are in good physical condition to begin with.
- It takes a bare minimum of five years military service to qualify for the Special Forces "Green Beret" (minimum rank of corporal / captain with airborne qualification, then a 1-2 year highly rigorous and selective training program.)
- It takes three years to achieve proficiency as a first level leader in an infantry unit—a squad leader.[152]

It is no less difficult to learn to fashion an elite, highly competitive company. Yet for some reason, otherwise intelligent people sometimes feel they should be able to attend a three-day seminar and return home experts in maneuver conflict as applied to business. An intensive orientation session may get you started, but successful leaders study their art for years—Patton, Rommel, and Grant were all known for the intensity with which they studied military history and current campaigns.

Then-LTC David Hackworth had commanded 10 other units before taking over the 4th Battalion, 39th Infantry in Vietnam in 1969, as he described in *Steel My Soldiers' Hearts*.

You may also recall the scene in *We Were Soldiers* where LTC Hal Moore unloaded armfuls of strategy and history books as he was moving into his quarters at Ft. Benning. At that point, he had been in the Army 20 years and had commanded at every level from platoon to battalion.

Once you know what you're doing, however, organizational change does not have to become a long and drawn out affair. If you have the requisite experience and put the organizational *Schwerpunkt* on building the proper climate, the pace of change may surprise you. Less than a month after assuming command of the Second Corps, decimated by Rommel at the Battle of Kasserine Pass (February 1943), Patton led it to victory on the Mareth Line, which broke the back of the Afrika Korps. It only took Hackworth about six weeks to turn the decrepit 4/ 39 into "Hardcore Recondos," who amassed one of the best combat records of the war and with remarkably few American casualties.

Spectacular turnarounds are still possible in the US airline industry, but it would require executives to abandon their fixations on cost cutting and instead become obsessed with installing competitive cultures. They would get their lower costs, but they would also see improved performance, more loyal customers, and better bottom line results. Southwest, as we have seen, does put the emphasis on tending the culture, and its average pre-tax return on revenue since 1979 has been 12.7%, compared to the Big 3's 0.6%[153] If adopting this culture and strategy is indeed the *Schwerpunkt* for your organization, then like a military commander, that is where you should place yourself. Ordering your subordinates to learn Boyd's strategy, without making it the focus of your own efforts, will rightly be viewed as the latest flavor-of-the-month sham.

A garden analogy may help summarize implementing Boyd's operational climate. The duty of senior managers is to design the garden, decide what they want to grow, and prepare the proper conditions. Obviously to do this well, they must be highly experienced gardeners, with a sure feel for the soil conditions, the nature of their plants, the climate, and the local rabbit population. Once conditions are right and seeds are in the ground, the plants grow themselves—bottom up, as Boyd used to emphasize. With seeds planted, and favorable climate and soil conditions, the "system" implements itself. The gardeners must work the plot, checking the condition of the plants, and always ensuring that conditions for growth are as favorable as possible—even a moment's inattention can mean disaster. And most important, weeds must be removed, no matter how tall they grow.[154]

CHAPTER VI

Surprise and Anticipation: The Real Principles of War, as Applied to Business

"Welch understands better than most the value of surprise." (of Jack Welch, Retired Chairman and CEO of General Electric)[155]

Order and Chaos

"We had nothing material to lose," wrote T. E. Lawrence (of Arabia) in *Seven Pillars of Wisdom*, "so our best line was to defend nothing and to shoot nothing. Our cards were speed and time, not hitting power." This is an amazing statement, a warrior throwing down his weapon and controlling the enemy purely by what strategists call "shaping his concept of the conflict."

Although Lawrence may represent an extreme case, shaping is a persistent theme of strategy of all types going back some 2,500 years.

The 17th century Samurai, Miyamoto Musashi, had taught 300 years before Lawrence that a samurai could win with any weapon, or with none at all, if he used strategy to prepare the opponent before the fight began. Good strategy defeats physical attributes in business as in war, except that in war we shape the enemy and move him as if we were also commanding his forces, and in business we shape and are shaped by the customer and marketplace.

The question is how to do it. As we have seen, considerable data support the notion that a critical ingredient in strategy, both military and commercial, is the ability to rapidly execute Boyd's OODA "loop." In particular, businesses that execute this loop more quickly than their competitors will have the major influence on shaping customers' perception of what is desirable.

Let's look at a way to use rapid OODA loop speed to shape the environment. We'll start, as usual, with war and then apply the same underlying ideas, but not the tactics or strategy, to business.

In Figure 17 all of the actions of the secondary units are geared to ensuring that the unit with the main focus succeeds in its flanking attack. Note that the schematic does not indicate the actual sizes of the forces. The secondary units may form our largest component, to engage the enemy (and his attention) while the main effort infiltrates unobserved to its intended objective. The *Nebenpunkte / Schwerpunkt* scheme works at all levels, so that troops and commanders from 10-person squads to 100,000 person corps shape their piece of the action through designating a main effort, often implicitly.

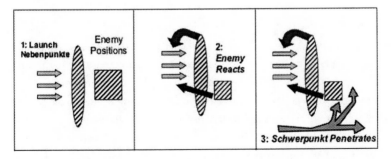

Figure 17—Simple Maneuver Scheme

It is worth repeating that in business, unlike in war, the main effort or focus is generally not a specific unit or division of the company. More often in business, the focusing device is a concept, like Microsoft's "trustworthy computing," that all the other activities of the company must support. In particular, it tells people, "Whenever you have a conflict or are unsure of what to do, take the action that best supports the main focus." However, a leader in a business still needs to be "at the *Schwerpunkt*," even a conceptual one.

A key idea of maneuver warfare is that once we have organized our strategic concept with a focusing main effort and auxiliary secondary efforts, we can play a special and powerful game known by its Chinese name: *cheng / ch'i*. It turns out that we can play this game in business, too, and with equally powerful results.

Don't Cheng Unless You Ch'i

Sun Tzu's goal was to shape the enemy's mind so that if armed conflict finally proved necessary, it would be relatively quick and bloodless. One of the primary tools for achieving this was the interplay between things he called *cheng* and *ch'i*. *Cheng* maneuvers are those that the enemy can comprehend: the formations lined up for battle, the chariots on the wings, the maneuvering and charging in full view of the enemy. Thus *cheng* is usually translated as something like "orthodox" or "expected." We might even add, "measurable." Experience suggests that if you try to force victory only through what can be observed and measured, that is, primarily through *cheng*, you will find yourself in attrition warfare.

You might expect that the complementary concept, *ch'i* maneuvers, are the unorthodox, unanticipated, irregular, surprising elements. You would be right: the charge that seems to come out of nowhere to strike at the rear; the sudden turning of 'defeated' troops to fire on their now disorganized pursuers—known as a "baited retreat," a favorite tactic of the Mongols and used with great effect by Daniel Morgan at the Cowpens during the American Revolution. As we saw above, Lawrence of Arabia carried on entire campaigns seemingly on *ch'i* alone.

Another View of Sun Tzu

The first translation of Sun Tzu that became popular in the West, and still outsells all others, was published by US Marine General Samuel B. Griffith in 1963 as an outgrowth of his doctoral thesis at Oxford. As an oriental scholar, as well as a practitioner of the art of war, Gen. Griffith offered a unique and valuable perspective on Sun Tzu's use of *cheng* and *ch'i*:

- Their (*cheng* and *ch'i*) effects are mutually generative and reinforcing
- One way to look at it is that *Cheng* = distraction; *ch'i* = decision (However it should be noted that neither by itself will have these effects.)
- *Ch'i* by definition represents the unexpected, strange, or unorthodox. (You can try a maneuver that you intend to be *ch'i*, but whether it actually is depends on the enemy. This is why preparing the enemy is so important in the Sun Tzu / Boyd school.)
- Engage with the *cheng*, win with the *ch'i*.
- *Cheng / ch'i* maneuvers apply to every one and every level within the organization.
- If the enemy, despite our best efforts, sees through our *ch'i* maneuver, then it would immediately become a *cheng*.[156]

Although there have been many translations since, notably the mellifluous prose of orientalist Thomas Cleary in 1988, which is the primary source for this book, Griffith and his commentary remain fascinating and essential reading for any strategist today.

Applying Deceit and Ambiguity

If *ch'i* maneuvers are so effective, one might wonder why have *cheng* at all? It's a good question, given the carnage that direct/*cheng* attacks have produced over the last 150 years. However, if you think only in terms of *ch'i*, reflect on the fact that relatively few pure guerilla movements actually succeeded. South Vietnam, for example, was finally conquered by the "People's Army," the regular army of North Vietnam, not the Viet Cong, who were severely reduced as a fighting force during the 1968 Tet Offensive. It was the North Vietnamese Army that Hal Moore fought at Ia Drang. Even Lawrence returned to more orthodox tactics as Allenby's right flank on the march on Damascus. It wasn't a demand for conformity by regular British commanders as much as Lawrence's own recognition that continued guerrilla warfare at that stage—no matter how successful—would reduce him to, as he put it, "a sideshow to a sideshow."

As the last bullet above shows, these are not aberrations. The enemy would quickly recognize a *ch'i*-only strategy and would expect it. It would thereby degrade into a *cheng*-only approach. In warfare, the two work together or not at all.

Another way to visualize this is that *cheng* are often the "pinning" forces used to engage the enemy at the start of the battle. *Ch'i* forces are often the "maneuver" forces, used to collapse the enemy's flanks and rear while the pinning/*cheng* forces have fixed the enemy's attention on the front. The end results of a properly executed *cheng*/*ch'i* maneuver include (on the enemy side) panic, chaos, fear, disintegration, shock, and so on. You can see how continued combat at this point might well not be required, or if it is, will be much easier and less costly in terms of people and material.

In business, the *ch'i* also needs the *cheng*: "Sell the sizzle not the steak," works great—until the customer tries the steak. Sun Tzu was careful to say that certain victory involves both *cheng* and *ch'i*. He goes on to explain that each contains ways to create the other, and that there is no limit to these combinations.[157]

In any competition, however, you have to assume that your competitors are as smart and as motivated as you are. We called this the "basic rule of all competition" in chapter IV, and it should still be burned into your mind. They know you are going to try to deceive and surprise them, so they are on the lookout for just those things. In war, unless we offer the enemy something to capture his attention, to convince him that his clever intelligence has seen through our nefarious schemes, he will continue probing our plans, trying to shape us. When he discovers our "*ch'i*" maneuver, it will instantly become *cheng* (since he has now seen through it), and if that's all we have, we're out of luck.

> *"Is there any point to which you would wish to draw my attention?"*
> *"To the curious incident of the dog in the nighttime."*
> *"The dog did nothing in the nighttime."*
> *"That was the curious incident," remarked Sherlock Holmes.*[158]

In other words, not seeing (and being engaged by) any *cheng*, Holmes kept looking for the *ch'i*, and he eventually found it.

What about the relation between the unorthodox (*ch'i*) and the main effort? The short answer, which will suit our purposes here, is that the unit carrying out the *ch'i* is the main effort, no matter how large or small it is. All other activities are *cheng*. Their purpose is to support the *ch'i* and do whatever they can to ensure it succeeds. Every secondary unit, however, must be prepared to become the main effort if the situation shifts it over to them.

Most readers are familiar with the dualities that seem to inhabit everything oriental, the best known being the *yin / yang*. *Yin* signifies such things as endurance and the maintenance of present states, while *yang* represents vitality and change.[159] In the Taoist cosmology that underlies eastern strategy, neither can exist without the other, and the familiar symbol shows each depending on and containing the seed of the other.

Figure 18—The Yin / Yang Duality

"Each contains the seeds of the other," means that each can become the other if conditions warrant. If *cheng* were always pinning and *ch'i* always flanking, as I have noted but it bears repeating, the scheme would not work at all. Any opponent worthy of the name would quickly detect that pattern and wouldn't he try to exploit our predictability, perhaps by ambushing our flanking forces? Now let's play the game of *cheng* and *ch'i*: Anticipating this, couldn't we try sending token forces around the flanks and then execute a surprise frontal assault (which would now be the *ch'i*, as in Figure 19)?

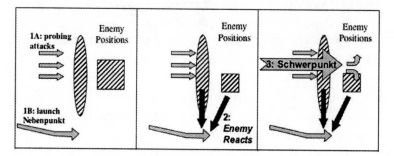

Figure 19—A Deceptive Maneuver Scheme

It worked for Col Emory Upton's brigade, whose direct frontal attack at Spotsylvania Courthouse on May 10, 1864, nearly collapsed Lee's line. Had he been supported according to plan, the Civil War might have ended a year earlier. Alexander the Great almost always launched his main attack, including himself, at the strongest part of the enemy line[160]

Even this doesn't capture the richness of the *cheng* / *ch'i* game, however, since we can maneuver in *time* as well as *space*. Boyd described "maneuvering in time" as jerking the enemy between menacing dilemmas until he comes unglued. As Marine Corps doctrine states (see the excerpt at the end of chapter III), the goal is to create confusion and panic and thereby collapse the enemy's will to resist.

Figure 19 illustrates how this might happen. Suppose the enemy for whatever reason expects us to use a frontal=*Nebenpunkte* / flank=*Schwerpunkt* scheme. If our unit has high OODA loop speed, we could start with the plan shown in Figure 19, above, send out a token flanking force (which would be the *cheng*, of course), sense the flow of battle, and if the flanking attack starts to succeed anyway, it would become the *ch'i* and the new main effort. In this case, we might rapidly funnel in reserves to reinforce this new *Schwerpunkt*. Or we might keep the original main effort, but delay the full force of our frontal attack until the flanking movement creates the appropriate level of chaos in the enemy's rear. The effect in any case will appear chaotic to the enemy, as the situation seems to change by the minute and our forces start appearing abruptly where they were not expected. There are infinitely many possible permutations; good maneuver warfare commanders do not fall into predictable patterns. As Col Wyly insisted, maneuver warfare is warfare without rules.[161]

Hitler, in perhaps the most famous incident of outsmarting oneself, was so sure that the Normandy invasion was a distraction (*cheng*), that as late as the first week in August (1944, after D-Day on June 6th), he was still withholding sizable forces to defeat what he was sure was a "*ch'i*" attack that would come across the Pas de Calais. Outsmarting oneself is also not uncommon in the murky game of intelligence, where it is not always clear whether what you uncovered is fact or what you were meant to uncover. It is said that this dilemma so captivated one CIA Director of Counterintelligence that the more valuable the information offered by a proposed defector, the more convinced Counterintelligence became that s/he was an enemy plant.[162]

Deceit and Ambiguity in Every Form of Competition

Like Sun Tzu, Boyd emphasized the primary role of *cheng/ch'i*:

- *Cheng / ch'i* maneuvers were employed by early commanders to expose adversary vulnerabilities and weaknesses (á la *cheng*) for exploitation and decisive stroke (via *ch'i*) [163]
- Use *cheng/ch'i* scheme to achieve an expenditure of energy or an irruption of violence—focused into, or through, features that permit an organic whole to exist[164]

- Establish focus of main effort (*ch'i* / *Schwerpunkt*) together with other related efforts (*cheng* / *Nebenpunkte*) and pursue directions that permit many happenings, offer many branches, and threaten alternative objectives (note: which ties multiple thrusts into the *cheng* / *ch'i* scheme)[165]
- The ultimate goal is to "generate uncertainty, confusion, disorder, panic chaos . . . to shatter cohesion, produce paralysis, and bring about collapse."[166]
- . . . to gain a feel for the different ways that the *cheng* / *ch'i* game has been (and can be) played[167]

Unlike Sun Tzu, Boyd examined all forms of human conflict, but his conclusion was the same: *cheng* / *ch'i* maneuvers are fundamental to any strategy for defeating your opponent.

Of course, if you want to dispense with strategy and try to pound him into oblivion (but even this might be a *ch'i* strategy, if the opponent were expecting you to maneuver), you don't need to worry about these things. Historically, however, the results of such "strategies" tend to be less than elegant: The US in Vietnam and Russia in Afghanistan and Chechnya are typical.

How to Ch'i *in Business*

Business is a form of Boydian conflict, as we have seen, so it should be that *cheng* / *ch'i* maneuvers apply there as well. But there is a big difference: In business, there are customers and competitors, but no enemy whose mind we are trying to cloud and spirit we are trying to weaken before we destroy him physically (if necessary). These are, of course, why we employ *cheng* / *ch'i* maneuvers in war.

To illustrate *cheng* and *ch'i* in business, let's consider what a pure *cheng* maneuver would be. Your first impression might be a frontal assault on the competition, while a *ch'i* would be some type of indirect approach. Immediately, though, we run into problems. We cannot "assault" competitors (at least not legally). Similarly, we cannot "defend" market share or a line of business from the competition. These are analogies and as such may be more or less illuminating—or misleading.

All we can do is go out into the marketplace and offer products and services. You can see now the difficulty trying to use military terminology when discussing other forms of conflict.

The key to understanding *cheng* and *ch'i* in business lies in looking carefully at the nature of the terms themselves rather at their specific applications in war. One of the main themes of this book has been that the essence of Boyd's strategy in business competition is to shape ourselves and the marketplace to improve our capacity for independent action—to survive on our terms—generally at the expense of our competitors. The nature of war is to shape the enemy. Detect a connection? The nature of *cheng / ch'i*, in both cases as it will turn out, is not "frontal versus flank" but something more fundamental: "shaping," using orthodox (expected) in conjunction with the unorthodox (surprising). Engage with the *cheng* and win with the *ch'i*, in business as in war.

"Cheng" = "Expected"

You would think that this means "works as advertised," but unfortunately, in much of business today, just working would be surprising, and so be *ch'i*. I can illustrate this by using the personal computer industry, where working as advertised would be absolutely shocking. This appears to be beyond the ability of computer executives to understand. If you use Windows, for example, you might have received a message like, "This program cannot be closed. If it is being debugged, close the debugger first." Does this mean anything to you? Do you think that Microsoft hands out copies of the code behind Word to its retail customers so that they can "debug" it?

It's an endemic problem, and Apple also has it. As I was trying today to backup a copy of a file on this Apple computer, I was greeted with: "CD Burning failed because an unknown fatal error occurred (-2147352480.)" The only button on the error box simply said, "OK." No, it is not "OK." If a company's product can't perform a simple task like burning a CD, it owes me more information than a 10-digit negative number and an idiotic button.

Why can't the people running computer companies understand that customers might resist the idea of laying out several thousand dollars for the privilege of being irritated and insulted by a machine? A common response to the question of "Why don't you replace that old piece of junk?" is "I'd like a new computer, but I finally got this one to work."

My guess is that computer executives don't spend much of their day out talking to typical customers.

Let's assume, despite lack of credible evidence, that someday personal computers will work as well as TVs and microwave ovens. At that point, "working as advertised" will indeed be *cheng*, and something else can become *ch'i*. In other words, there will be diminishing payoff to raising reliability from .999 to .9999 and somebody will have to come up with something other than product quality to sell hardware and software.

This is how the Japanese conquered the US car market in the '70s and '80s. Remember that the Japanese invasion enjoyed only limited success until the twin oil shocks of the 1970s. As a result of the quadrupling of gasoline prices, many people bought Japanese, expecting to get very good gas mileage, which they did. If this had been all, in other words, if the Japanese had only met their expectations, we would have predicted that once gas prices subsided, people would go back to Detroit iron.

In fact, the period of greatest Japanese success was the following decade. During the 1980s, for example, General Motors' US market share went from 52% to around 30%, with most of this lost to the Japanese. What happened? Ask anyone who bought a Honda, Toyota, or Datsun (as Nissan products were known until 1984) back then. They came expecting to get great gas mileage, which they did, but, "Surprise!" The things ran like a Swiss watch, fit together like a Rolls Royce, and seemed to last forever. In the language of strategy, the Japanese engaged with the expected (*cheng*)—gas mileage—but won with the unexpected (*ch'i*): fit and finish, driveability, longevity. Contrast this with GM's economy offerings of the period, the Vega and Chevette. Their gas mileage was as good as the Japanese, but in all other aspects, they were pretty ordinary. All *cheng*; no *ch'i*. Market share cut by 40%.

Ch'i: *The Magical Difference*

"Today people expect product quality," says Gary Powell, general manager for global quality at GE Plastics. "The area that becomes a differentiator is service."[168] This is progress, at least compared to the computer industry, but it still says something about the state of the marketplace that good service should be considered "surprising and unorthodox."

Apparently it is true and a prime modern example is Wal-Mart. They do the expected well: low prices, clean stores, and convenient locations. They have invested heavily in information systems, even to the point of launching their own satellite, to ensure that customers get what they expect. But, they also do the unexpected. They greet you at the door. Displays are clean and imaginatively arranged. They feature the latest merchandise. People usually act like they're having fun.

In modern American retailing, these are *ch'i* sorts of things. Their purpose is to turn a visit to Wal-Mart from a shopping trip into an experience that keeps you coming back. The challenge for Wal-Mart will come when we grow to expect these "unexpected" things, that is, when they become *cheng* instead of *ch'i*.

In addition to Wal-Mart, Disney and Southwest Airlines come to mind as practitioners of *cheng / ch'i*. Think of what happens when you are deciding to buy their products and services. You expect them to work as advertised—parades and planes on time, for example. Let me repeat that: You *expect* them to work. This defines *cheng* in their businesses, doing well what the customer expects, things like quality in terms of "free from defects," low price, good performance. A pure *cheng* approach to business would insist that these are enough. If you read any texts on marketing or strategy, particularly those that have the word "value" in the title, this is what you will get: the company that can best deliver "value" wins.

Both Disney and Southwest seem to understand that this is not enough. Southwest, for example, sends you birthday cards, and then there's their irreverent approach to life in general. Disney has sophisticated adult restaurants and pubs for after the kids go to bed. The challenge for both of these companies will be keeping the level of expectation (*cheng*) high, while still inventing unexpected things to delight us.

If "*cheng* = quality, *ch'i* = service" is too simplistic, and it is, what about equating *ch'i* to something like "glamour"? Even this fails to capture the richness of the *cheng / ch'i* game, for there is often money to be made by looking at the market from another angle. Porsche, for example, stands for the ultimate in a prestige sports car. Until recently, however, their quality left a lot to be desired. In other words, people expected panache and performance, and they got it, but that was all.

As a result, by 1993, Porsche's total production was down to 14,000 cars, about 25% of their peak in 1986, this despite the fact that the cars' performance was as good as ever and gas was cheap. In 1991, at the insistence of the Porsche family, a new general manager was named who instituted a crash program[169] to install Japanese-style production techniques in this most German of auto plants. Quality (defect rate) improved by approximately a factor of 10. Customers who bought Porsches still got the glamour and performance they expected, but now were delighted with the cars' quality. By 1995, sales were up about 50% over 1993.[170]

The Japanese have even divided quality itself into *cheng* and *ch'i* components. There is "defect free" quality, which is what the customer expects—*cheng*, of course. But recall from chapter IV that there is also *miriyoku teke hinshitsu*, or the quality that delights, which is pure "*ch'i*."

Think Cheng/Ch'i *from the Beginning*

By viewing conflict in terms of a *cheng / ch'i* symbiosis, you can break what would seem to be the trade-off between them. You don't cut back on your "expected" maneuvers in order to do more of the unexpected. An intelligent enemy would quickly notice such a pattern. What produces the effect is not *cheng* itself or *ch'i*, but the interplay between them. In maneuver warfare, commanders use their quick OODA loops to make rapid switches between the two and so produce the jerky, abrupt transitions that cause an enemy to hesitate and his ability to function to break down. In business, this interplay produces the customer delight that leads to brand loyalty and higher returns.

As you might have surmised from all of the above, using *cheng / ch'i* to advantage requires a lot more than "focus on the customer." That may get you *cheng*, but rarely *ch'i*. Tom Peters wrote a book back in 1994 whose title, *The Pursuit of WOW!* sums it all up. In the introduction, he complained that

> *I'm repeatedly struck by the parade of "new" cars that look like every other car, by how many newly opened French restaurants or just-launched PCs or software packages fail to zap you, by how one Big Six audit service resembles all the others.* [Author's note: this was written pre-Enron & Arthur Anderson]

Yet, the vast majority of these came from focusing on the customer: market research, focus groups, customer surveys, and the like. *Ch'i*, on the other hand, requires that mystical feel that we have called intuitive knowledge (*Fingerspitzengefühl*), which in business includes an ability to sense what will cause customers to become fascinated by our products and services. In other words, what will delight potential customers enough to keep them coming back to us and paying a premium for the privilege? For a company in a competitive marketplace, searching for answers to this question must be what gives you focus and direction.

Developing a Sense of Ch'i

Like a feel for the battle, one develops a sense of *ch'i* and how to play it with *cheng* through practice, study, contemplation, discussion, triumph, and failure. Most people can develop it but either don't recognize the need or won't take the time or they work for companies that don't value it. Musashi offers the best description of proper training that I know of in his *Book of Five Rings*. Musashi's particular field, fighting to the death with Japanese swords, is not much in demand today, but his method for honing a feel for competition until it seems magical applies to anything.

His method begins by working with the sword, doing basic exercises until the weapon becomes virtually an extension of the student's arm. This is like technical excellence—learning to do the expected well.

Musashi is clear at many places in his book that although such expected excellence is essential, it is not the key to victory. You cannot become so technically proficient that you are assured of winning every fight: If you achieved a 97% chance of winning a fight, which would be spectacular against people who train just as hard as you do, your odds of surviving 25 fights is less than 50%. Musashi won 60 duels, so clearly he was not thinking of taking that kind of risk. He wanted no risk at all.[171]

For that, one needs to develop an ability to do the unexpected and then exploit its result quickly. The key to this strategy is a different type of training, where students practice generating *ch'i* and using it with *cheng* as instinctively as they previously practiced manipulating the sword. The training gradually becomes more realistic so that finally they face the real chance of injury or death.[172]

If you want to develop a sense for what might be *ch'i* in your business, you first need to recognize the need for *ch'i*, set up by **the** *cheng*, as the (not "an") instrument of decision in all forms of competition.

Not Just a Nice-To-Have

Boyd insisted that "*ch'i*" and "*Schwerpunkt*" are essentially the same, that is, *finding and exploiting the magical element should be what gives your enterprise focus and direction.*

Just admitting this simple possibility goes against the culture of most US companies whose managers take pride in being "hard-nosed realists," demanding studies and "proofs" before committing. It is easy to use these weapons to stifle new initiatives, since *ch'i* as the unorthodox/ surprising component by definition cannot be proven beforehand. Unfortunately, the products of such companies usually reflect this attitude. You might take the words of the late W. Edwards Deming, which opened chapter II, to heart: "He who would run his business with visible figures alone will soon have neither business nor visible figures to work with."

The idea of *ch'i* as the *Schwerpunkt* also illustrates how businesses can at times have more than one focusing concept. The main emphasis of the Toyota *Production* System, for example, is on constantly reducing the order-to-delivery span. This concept is not, however, a suitable focus for Toyota as a company, since it doesn't say anything about what car to deliver in a shorter time span. In other words, if shorter order-to-deliver were all, Toyota would still be building better and better 1976 Camrys, faster and faster.

What they actually do is try to design cars people want to buy, and then the production system will build them faster, with better quality, and at lower cost than the competition. It is the job of top management to sense what the public wants to buy, even if the public doesn't realize it, yet. The development system will design and engineer it quickly (compared to Detroit) and ensure that the production system can build it. So there really are two separate *Schwerpunkts*—the development system is not a *Nebenpunkt* and the Production System the *Schwerpunkt*, for example—but, and this is the key point, they are harmonized to try to sense the marketplace, conceptualize what the public will buy, design and produce it more quickly than the competition, and then learn from the experience. Quicker OODA loops, in the language of maneuver conflict.

As a result of the harmonized system, Toyota can deliver their expected high quality, *cheng*, and also try to infuse enough surprise, delight, enchantment, that is, sufficient *ch'i*, to sell the car in the first place. Having the *cheng* down pat, they can put their energy into finding and exploiting the *ch'i*.

In warfare, one purpose of using *cheng / ch'i* is to generate the jerky, abrupt, unexpected and disorienting changes that Boyd called "asymmetric fast transients." We could generate such an effect, for example, when we spring the *ch'i* on an opponent whose attention has been captured by the *cheng* and so believes that he understands the situation. There is a similar-sounding term in business strategy called "market dislocation," an innovation so profound that it changes the rules of the game in that market segment. The Internet is often cited as such a dislocation, and the theory is that we should be the ones striving to unleash such dislocations.

Perhaps, although there are some caveats. Most innovations fail in the marketplace. Even when they succeed, it is often not the inventor who makes the money, as we have noted before, but the ones who best adapt it to fit what customers will buy. So dislocation might better be visualized as a process rather than as an event. Many dislocations, in fact, are abrupt only when viewed through the distortion of time. Ten years after its introduction, for example, the Internet is now becoming a significant factor in global commerce, and last year was the first that such pure plays as eBay and Amazon made any money.

Part of the problem with thinking in terms of dislocations is that we do not have, nor will anyone ever have, the ability to dislocate the market. As Boyd reminded his audiences, we cannot surprise or deceive the enemy, either. All we can do in any of these cases is use our experience, judgment, and intuition to try things, observe what happens, and keep trying things. Surprise, deception, and dislocation are the intended effects, but whether they work is up to the enemy or to customers.

A better way to regard *ch'i* in business is the look of amazement and delight on the faces of customers when they discover magic in our products. Like the "What the f__k!" reaction of less agile fighter pilots, it's "Incredible! Hey honey, look at this!" It's the emotional force that pulls customers to do more business with us, and to tell their friends. Using "Ok, everything works."/*cheng* in combination with "This is so cool!"/*ch'i* is as fundamental to success in business as employing Nebenpunkte/*cheng* to set up Schwerpunkt/*ch'i* is to maneuver warfare.

No probabilities here; you've made yourself certain to win.

Do You Really Want to Stare Death in the Face?

What about putting yourself into situations where you could be injured or killed? Musashi insisted that practice imitate the real world as closely as possible. The Zen masters of Musashi's age emphasized the ultimate role of objective reality, and much of their practice was designed to minimize the possibility that one's existing orientation would cloud one's perception—the risk in that "implicit guidance and control" link from orientation back to observation (see Figure 20 in the Appendix.) The link is there, apparently hardwired into our physiology, and cannot be wished away. The question is how can we, as practitioners of *The Way of Business*, ensure that it does not mislead us, that we don't start believing our own propaganda?

One way, as mentioned earlier, is to take active measures to seek out and reward bearers of bad news, the corporate versions of Sun Tzu's spies. Here's another, even simpler idea: Be the customer. I don't mean "identify with the customer," or "respond to customer desires," or some other inane canard. All business is people buying from people. You're on the selling side, so to understand what happens on the buying side, walk around the table and sit in the buyer's seat. If you're in retail of some type, buy your own product or service just the way the paying public does and use it just they way they do.

Delta Airlines' slogan for many years was, "Delta gets you there." One should certainly hope so, placing this curious marketing pitch into the category of pure *cheng*. So let's pick on the airline industry. If you're a high roller with some airline, call your 1-800 telephone number to make a reservation. Try your web site. Stand in line to check in. Check a suitcase. Fly coach. Try to change a reservation. What do you think? Excited by your own stuff? Any sign of magical pizzazz there? Any reason anybody with a choice would do it again? And while you're back there in coach, talk to people. Don't limit your observations to fishing for what's wrong, since that's a shortfall in meeting their expectations. Important stuff, but *cheng*, not *ch'i*. You have to be much more subtle and creative. Somewhere there's a spark, some "Eureka!" that will cause people to choose you over Continental or even Southwest and pay more to do it.

I have no idea what it is, although Herb Kelleher at Southwest seems to have a good lead on figuring it out. After all, I'm not getting in the high six figures as an airline exec, but I can recognize it if and when they put it in. So will you. There may be a glimmer of hope for the industry since some of the new low-cost airlines, particularly JetBlue, seem to be trying for a little *ch'i* in the form of leather seats and video systems in addition to the expected low fare *cheng*.

Another piece of advice: Improve your skill at many-sided implicit cross referencing by sharing the bits and pieces you discover, as well as any conclusions you are coming to, by using the three primary pipelines of modern knowledge management. These are e-mail and instant messaging, your corporate intranet, and hanging around the office water cooler and coffee pot.[173] An occasional happy hour wouldn't hurt, either (don't let people drive home drunk.)

It is harder, I admit, in some industries, particularly if you sell to institutions. Solving this problem, though, is why corporate executives get the big bucks. For example, if you can't be the customer, at the very least, you can spend a lot of time one-on-one with them. Another idea: Who in your own company makes buying decisions? Can you rotate into one of those shops? If you sell internationally, you can invite energetic personalities from target countries to serve on your board. There are no rules in strategy, so be creative.

Clearness of Vision Precedes Clarity of Thought

Which bring us to our last point. Sun Tzu and his successors, including John Boyd, have all emphasized interaction with the outside world—perception/appreciation—as central to strategy. Boyd observed that "appreciation includes the recognition of worth or value and the idea of clear perception . . . it is difficult to believe that leadership can even exist without appreciation." The Japanese Zen philosopher/warriors considered failure to achieve "right perception" or "fluid awareness" as a sickness[174], which must be cured before the true study of strategy can begin. In this regard, an obvious purpose of "Be the Customer!" is to open up your perception.

There is more. Becoming the customer will tell you if *ch'i* is already there, and it is really good at detecting problems in *cheng* (where reality falls short of expectation). What about ideas for creating *ch'i* in the first place, those aspects of a product or service that, as Peters characterizes it, take your breath away? Where do these come from?

The subject of creativity and innovation—for *ch'i*, as the unexpected, requires a timely creative act—has fascinated strategists for years. I can't tell you from where you will get great inspirations. One thing for sure, the spark of *ch'i* is unlikely to arise from talking with the same old people about the same old things day in and day out. Recall the advice from the ultimate samurai, Musashi: "Pursue the arts," and "Practice the crafts." Or Peters' advice to put down the same management text everyone else is reading (including his!) and study human nature through novels and biography.

Why? Because you never know what will prod your creativity, and the more widely you prospect, the more likely you are to find that something to set your offerings apart from all of your competitors. Toyota claims that the idea for their amazing production system came from engineers who visited supermarkets in the United States after the war. Studies of innovation reveal that practically everything new consists of bits and pieces of other concepts, often from fields that appeared to be unrelated, that somebody had the genius to reassemble to form something new and exciting.

Boyd called this, "building snowmobiles," from an observation that a snowmobile is made up from pieces of other things (treads from a tractor, engine from an outboard motor, etc.) that someone in a spark of creativity visualized could be ripped apart and put back together to serve this new purpose. His final "Metaphorical Message" was that

> *A winner is someone (individual or group) that can build snowmobiles, and employ them in an appropriate fashion, when facing uncertainty and unpredictable change.*

The Way Ahead

The purpose of this chapter has been to introduce the *cheng / ch'i* concept and illustrate its power. As for implementation, experience suggests that employing *cheng / ch'i* requires the creativity and judgment of all the people in the organization. It seems reasonable that you're more likely to capture something truly original if you have more people looking. You'll do even better if, once people find an idea for *ch'i*, they can act on it. It's the commercial version of multiple thrusts and reconnaissance pull. Unfortunately, the schematics shown in Figures 17 and 19 may give the impression that strategy is best carried out by a single controlling intelligence on each side, much as in a game of chess. In this view, the functions of the other players are simply to execute orders. Although such systems may enjoy an initial success against unprepared opponents, the historical record suggests that this *"führer* principle" mainly serves to destroy the organization employing it. Lord Acton's famous dictum[175] is not easily thwarted.

Now it is true that successful military organizations are not participatory democracies. There is a commander, and his or her intent is paramount and orders must be obeyed. Highly effective military organizations, however, have found ways to harmonize the commander's intent with the initiatives of all the other members of the organization— which is the ultimate force multiplier. By using a climate like Boyd's from chapters III and V, they have broken the tradeoff between organizational harmony and individual initiative. A good place to look for further ideas is in Marine Corps Doctrine Publication (MCDP) 1, *Warfighting*. Despite its formidable title, it spends most of its space on issues like harmonizing efforts, making decisions in the face of uncertainty, and always keeping the initiative,[176] things that apply to business as much as they do to war.

Even if there were The Perfect Solution for you, if someone handed it to you, it wouldn't work. Instead, put yourself at the *Schwerpunkt* of the transformation effort. Look people in the eyes when you're preaching the new doctrine. Lead your company in studying Sun Tzu and Musashi, discussing *Warfighting*, and comparing your processes to those of Toyota. Start your own Crotonville and teach there yourself. If you must have staff meetings, devote at least part of them to building a common awareness of the principles in the fundamental works of maneuver conflict and constantly filter all your activities through the *cheng / ch'i* lens, remembering that the *ch'i* must always be the focus of your main efforts. That, and a healthy sense of urgency, will give you a fighting chance at evolving a winning organization (which may well end up looking nothing like Toyota, the USMC, or anything else anyone has ever seen). And always remember the mantra: promote those who do, remove those who do not.

We may conclude with the claim that success in any competitive endeavor requires attention to both the expected and the unexpected. Engage with the *cheng*, close with the *ch'i*. One of the reasons that the socialist economic system failed was concentration on the expected *cheng*—which is the best you get from centralized planning—with a puritan disdain for the delightful *ch'i*. We dimly remember the loud and smoky Trabant and block after block of shoddy gray apartment complexes. The sad fact is that many US companies today seem dedicated to keeping the socialist central planning model alive, with the results reflected in their products and services. By 1990, the people of Eastern Europe had finally had enough and overthrew (with astoundingly little violence) the second greatest military power in history. You have it easy.

CHAPTER VII

What You Really Do with OODA Loops

I don't want to get any messages saying, "I am holding my position."
We are not holding a Goddamned thing. Let the Germans do that. We
are advancing constantly and we are not interested in holding onto
anything, except the enemy's *******. Gen George S. Patton, Jr.[177]

We're Not Holding Anything

One often reads that the purpose of quick OODA loop speed has
to do with "responding rapidly to changing market conditions" or some
such. If after reading this far you still have this notion, then I have
failed. Boyd's concept of strategy is vastly more powerful, and hearkens
back to the days when conflict truly was the path of life and death:

- Uncover, create, and exploit many vulnerabilities and weaknesses,
  hence many opportunities, to pull adversary apart and isolate
  remnants for mop-up or absorption

- Generate uncertainty, confusion, disorder, panic, chaos . . . to shatter cohesion, produce paralysis and bring about collapse
- Destroy the moral bonds (of the enemy) that permit an organic whole to exist
- Create moral bonds that permit us, as an organic whole, to shape and adapt to change[178]

With a strategy this powerful, your aim is not to respond to but to create the market conditions that you want.

The mechanics for doing this depend on the specific market you are in, although all marketplaces share common characteristics that Boyd's strategy can exploit. In particular, markets, like so many systems involving humans, are "complex," a technical term which means, *inter alia*, that they are not predictable using the methods of formal mathematics and simulation. Complex systems do exhibit patterns, however, and places like the Santa Fe Institute have accumulated a considerable body of knowledge about how these systems behave. If you are in business, the marketplace is your playing field, so it stands to reason that you need to build an intuitive sense for how complex systems work.

A good place to start is Stephen Wolfram's book, *A New Kind of Science*. Wolfram shows that all complex systems are in a sense equivalent to a simple type of system known as a "cellular automata," and his company even sells a program that will let you experiment with them yourself. All the complexity in the real world can be generated, Wolfram shows, by the repeated action of these "simple machines." Complexity is the norm in the world, he concludes, and arises naturally as randomness "self-organizes" (also a term Boyd also liked) into the patterns generated by simple systems acting over time.[179] The systems, in other words, are simple, but there is no limit to the complexity they can generate, given enough time.

Now, here is the interesting part: The OODA loop is a simple machine. It can generate all the strategic "patterns of conflict" that can exist in the world. It not only adapts to the complexity of the marketplace, it has the power to harmonize with and help shape the marketplace.

The key, as we have seen, is the ability to manipulate time, that is, quickness. This also fits with the idea of a simple machine, since it may take many operations of such a machine to generate a complex pattern, and so time becomes the critical parameter.

Quickness, as we know, depends upon the climate in which the OODA loop operates, and a particularly effective climate for this is the one we have called the "key attributes of the blitzkrieg": mutual trust/unity/cohesion, intuitive knowledge; mission contract/orders; and focus of effort. This climate isn't implemented so much as it grows naturally under conditions where people study it, embrace it, and those who use it are rewarded and those who do not are removed.

I've Got It, Now What?

It depends on what type of conflict you want to shape. If it is armed conflict—war—then use maneuver warfare itself. It has been widely studied and its results are incontrovertible. If your business involves manufacturing, use the Toyota Production System, which is as close as we have come to the Way, or *Tao*, of Manufacturing, and it contains within itself mechanisms to nudge it ever closer. Like classic maneuver warfare, the techniques for employing it are well understood, and the results equally clear: those that adopt the TPS drive their competitors from the marketplace. There is also a Toyota Development System that is based on the same principles and delivers similar results. To the best of my knowledge, these are the only three implementations of maneuver conflict principles so far.

If your business does not fall into one of these categories, you will have to do some of the adapting yourself. There may well be a Way of Airline Management, but there is of yet no Toyota Airline System or even a sales system that people recognize as lean. The principles of maneuver conflict, however, help groups of people work together under conditions of stress and uncertainty to shape their environments and their futures, and this describes any modern business.

Regardless of the specific business you are in, here are some ideas you may find useful.

Keep Your Focus on Shaping the Marketplace

This means that you want to be the one who defines and continues to define what "new and desirable" means. You will extract the industry's highest margins and often make money even when the market is bad. Because you won't be so much at the mercy of lenders and the markets, you can preserve your capacity for independent action, survive on your own terms, and, as Toyota insisted, take control of your own destiny.

It is not a one-sided relationship, however. Only customers' votes get counted, and they look at what you offer, what your competitors offer, the other things to spend money on, and somehow factor in their opinion of your company, your competitors, the state of the economy, their sense of style, and God knows what else. Just like you do when you're buying something. Using the *cheng / ch'i* concept, you can help shape and be shaped by all of this, but you cannot reliably plan it. As Boyd pointed out, a plan is only an intention, and a strategy is merely a scheme for creating and managing plans.

Since business is a competition, you don't have to be perfect, only better than everyone else.

But You Probably Won't Win Just by Doing the Same Old Things Better Than Everybody Else

The Toyota Production System, in other words, is not General Motors where somebody has gone down the aisles and "removed all the waste." The TPS is an implementation of maneuver conflict principles, but conventional push-type production is not. So what do you do if you're not in one of the industries that already has an implementation of maneuver conflict? The answer, apparently, is that once you pass some threshold of implementation, you begin to see the benefits and can be enormously competitive. Although there may be no Toyota Airline System, this has not kept Southwest Airlines from being the most profitable US major year in and year out and the only one to make money in 2002. Southwest, as we have seen, has adopted many of the principles of maneuver conflict, including a focus on time and an obsession with tending the culture.

In many ways, Southwest is not simply an improved version of Delta or United. You can tell this because both of these tried to create imitations of Southwest, down to only flying one type of aircraft, and they both failed miserably.[180] As an even partial implementation of maneuver conflict, Southwest has advantages the others cannot match, but these are, as co-founder Herb Kelleher notes, echoing Boyd and Sun Tzu (perhaps unintentionally), more cultural than physical.

The need for a change in underlying assumptions is what distinguishes maneuver conflict in all its forms from activities like "business process reengineering." As a result of implementing maneuver conflict, many of the existing processes and the relationships between them are going to disappear, and so it would be a waste of time and money to "improve" them. This breaking of relationships ("shattering of domains," as Boyd referred to it) is a prerequisite to implementing maneuver conflict, which is one reason why all successful implementations have eliminated roughly 25-40% of management positions, since those reflect the existing processes and relationships.

Make Time the Focus

This is the technique Toyota uses—continually reduce the time span measured from customer order to customer delivery, including the time required to inspect and fix (which will be zero if none is required, of course.)

You won't get there by trying to do the same stuff, only faster. What you'll get is a mess—every system runs at its characteristic speed for a given set of inputs. If you want your system to run faster, what you have to do is change it in ways that decrease the time it takes to do the most important things you do, those that affect the customer. Toyota, for example, is interested in reducing the time from order to delivery, and that is essentially the only time span they worry about. There would be no point or payoff in accelerating an individual activity if this would throw the whole system out of balance.

Growing Ideas

Boyd's own presentations, particularly *Patterns of Conflict, Organic Design for Command and Control,* and *Strategic Game of ? and ?* are available on Defense and the National Interest, *http:// www.d-n-i.net.* All of Boyd's works, with the exception of his early paper, "Destruction and Creation," are briefings and were never intended to stand on their own. They are worth downloading, however, and will repay careful study as you accumulate experience with maneuver conflict.

Tom Peters is, without any doubt, the management author most closely aligned with Boyd's philosophy. *Thriving on Chaos,* as I mentioned in the Preface, was the catalyst for concluding that the Toyota Production System and maneuver warfare are both implementations of the principles of maneuver conflict. *The Pursuit of WOW!* (1994) could as easily have been titled *A Field Guide to Ch'i,* and Peters' latest, *Re-imagine!* contains several sections on Boyd. All of these would be good additions to your library.

Once you're familiar with the basics of maneuver conflict theory, study the other implementations, particularly the Toyota Production System itself. It makes no difference whether you're in manufacturing or not, if you understand something about maneuver warfare and about the TPS, you will have seen the two most complete manifestations of these principles. And they are quite different. You might start with the book by the creator of the system, Taiichi Ohno.[181] This little volume, only 130 pages, is written in a cryptic, condensed style, much like the *Art of War,* and like Sun Tzu, must be read and mulled over many times.

You can certainly study the Toyota Development System, although there is much less documentation on it. You can also go back into the roots of maneuver warfare and the TPS/TDS, the *ur-source* of maneuver strategy: the Taoist and Zen masterpieces beginning with the *Tao Te Ching* and *The Art of War* and continuing to the present day (*Zen and the Art of Motorcycle Maintenance,* for example.) This would be an excellent idea, by the way, as would enrolling in Zen classes. As a preliminary, you could study Thomas

Cleary's introduction to Sun Tzu's *Art of War* and his commentary on strategy in *The Japanese Art of War*, both of which develop the Zen elements in strategy.

One source of techniques applicable to industries outside the Toyota systems is James Womack's and Daniel Jones' *Lean Thinking*. It is a strange and difficult book, weak in terms of underlying strategy, but so full of ideas that everybody should study it. Womack and Jones participated in the original studies that documented that the Toyota Production System was fundamentally different from current US auto manufacturing systems and that it worked.[182]

They probably know the mechanics of the TPS as well as anybody who has not managed a Toyota plant, and they understand how powerful it is. It was tempting to apply concepts from the TPS to practically every other form of human endeavor. But the TPS is just what it claims to be, a *production* system, designed for the repetitive manufacture of previously designed articles. When you try to apply this particular manifestation of maneuver conflict to other activities, you get chapters like, "A Channel for the Stream, a Valley for the Channel." You would arrive at similar results by trying to apply maneuver warfare directly to the problems of business.

The weakness in the book is that there is no recognition that the TPS is based on a deeper set of principles that do apply to other human activities, like warfare. The index is devoid of such basic terms as trust, cohesion, initiative, or even "maneuver," which was adopted as official USMC doctrine seven years before *Lean Thinking* appeared and so was hardly esoteric when that book was written. Without a climate like the one I have described in this book you will find it difficult to create a company capable of employing the ideas Womack and Jones present.

One book that does acknowledge that something basic forms the underpinning for competitive strategy is *Competing Against Time*, by George Stalk, Jr., and Tom Hout. There is a diagram and exposition, for example, of the OODA loop starting on page 180, although there is no discussion of underlying maneuver principles and how these determine OODA loop speed. This is still the best single book, though, on the application of time-based competition in business—nothing better has appeared since 1990. You will find it invaluable in convincing doubting Thomases, and again, I would suggest it to any strategist.

Finally, I'd like to recommend Gary Klein's books on intuition and intuitive decision making, *Sources of Power* (1998) and *Intuition at Work* (2003.) As you know by this point, intuitive methods, which Boyd included under the concept of *Fingerspitzengefühl*, form an integral part of his strategy. Klein's research has documented these effects and he describes ways to improve them in organizations.

How Do We Know That It's Working?

The most accurate indicator that you are starting to do maneuver conflict is that long established tradeoffs get broken. For example, in the TPS, it was the tradeoff between quality and cost (older systems could improve quality only by more inspections or more expensive components, both of which increased costs.) In maneuver warfare, it was primarily the trade between control from the top and initiative from the bottom (in earlier forms of warfare, more control meant less initiative.) Southwest Airlines seems to have found a way to break the relationship between customer service and cost—they have the lowest costs (highest productivity) and generally the best customer service in the business.

After a while, you should start noticing other indicators, like the "string of luck" that seemed to accompany early successes of the Blitzkrieg, an increase in customer loyalty, and of course, the ability to generate healthy margins, even when the economic climate is bad.

As Close As Can Be to a Formula

If you absolutely must have a formula, try this:

- **Study:** the principles of maneuver conflict; the known implementations (TPS, TDS, and maneuver warfare); partial implementations (Dell, Southwest Airlines, GE, etc.); the nature of complex systems; Zen. If you're not former military, join the Marine Corps.[183]
- **Institute leadership,** to quote Deming. In this case, it means to

promote those who embrace it and remove those who do not. It also means that the CEO must become the pope of the new religion, and note that "pope" is a full-time job.

- **Practice and experiment:** You don't learn any form of maneuver conflict, or any other martial art (for that is what maneuver conflict is) just from reading about it.

- **Share what you've learned:** formally via a "Crotonville" for your organization; informally via every mechanism you can think of—your intranet, staff meetings, around the water cooler and coffee pot, your own preaching as you ride the circuit. As Musashi insisted, study is a lifelong undertaking.[184]

- Every now and then, **transcend the boundaries.** Every successful implementation seems to have such a mechanism, from the military's "dinings in" to Herb Kelleher's chicken suit to the celebrations the Japanese throw to recognize their successes.

I would like to end with a description of how Boyd's strategy, fully implemented, might work in a company. The following was contributed by Col Mike Wyly, USMC, whom we have met many times in this book. After his Marine Corps career, he consulted for a while, and for the last 10 years has run a successful small business, the Bossov Ballet Theater. This description echoes his portrait of maneuver warfare that appears in "Thinking Like Marines":

> *This is business by people who have studied to learn the art of working together. It is business by people who share a code of honor that binds them in mutual trust. It is business whose purpose is as much to know its market—the attitudes and desires of the people who might buy its product or its service—as it is to provide that product or service with integrity. It is business by people who have formed an effective team that can act and that will act swiftly and decisively to seize an opportunity, even when the opportunity arises unexpectedly.*

The team is not set in its ways, except in its way of doing business, which is trust of one another within the company, integrity of its product and service, appreciation of the market and potential market, and the ability to act quickly. The tempo with which the team acts, adjusts, corrects, seeks opportunity, and acts upon it, is greater than the speed of which its competitors are capable. It is greater and more powerful than the market can resist, and in that way, it wins its customers.[185]

APPENDIX

Figure 20 overleaf

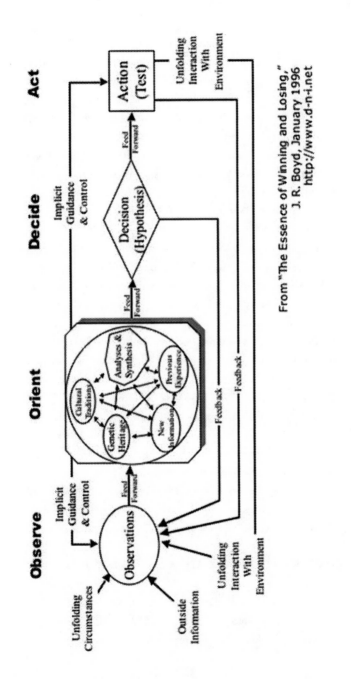

From "The Essence of Winning and Losing,"
J. R. Boyd, January 1996
http://www.d-n-i.net

Preface

[1] Samuel B. Griffith translation, Chapter I, Article 15.

[2] The six of the seven largest US airlines (excluding Southwest) lost $5.3 billion in 2003 (*Aviation Week*, March 1, 2004, p. 42). The final numbers for the whole US airline industry will be certified by the US Department of Commerce in June 2004. Figures for 2001 and 2002 include the $5 billion payments authorized by Congress to compensate for 9/11. Source is the Air Transport Association web site, *http://www.airlines.org*. Delta's loss will probably run close to one billion dollars, although extraordinary items will bring the number down to under $800 million. Southwest continued to make money in 2003, and some of the smaller airlines, including AirTran and JetBlue, were also profitable throughout this period.

[3] Ray L. Smith and Bing West, *The March Up*, p. 11.

[4] Those familiar with Boyd's work will recognize that I have taken liberties with his terminology. In *Patterns of Conflict*, the term "maneuver conflict" refers to one of his three categories of conflict; attrition warfare and moral conflict are the other two. I am going to use "maneuver conflict," however, to refer to the set of concepts that make up Boyd's philosophy of conflict. In that sense, "maneuver conflict" would be an alternative to something like "Boydism" or "Boydian conflict." Implementations of this philosophy in the field of war will generally be referred to as "maneuver warfare" (which would include both the Blitzkrieg and modern guerilla warfare), while the Toyota Production and Development Systems represent instances of it in the world of commerce. Interestingly, while Boyd is best known in military circles as a proponent of maneuver warfare, that phrase does not appear in *Patterns of Conflict*.

Chapter I Nor the Battle to the Strong

[5] The medieval commentator Zhang Yu, in Sun Tzu's *Art of War*, trans. Thomas Cleary, Boston: Shambhala, 1988, p. 56. Zhang is included in the standard collection of interpreters of Sun Tzu.

6   Simpler in the sense that at the strategic level, it consists of two sides engaged in a situation where gain to one is loss to the other. For our purposes, it can be represented by a two-person, zero-sum game. At the level of the individual participants, however, there is probably no more complex human activity than war.

7   The word simply means "armor," and is related to the English "paunch."

8   Boyd's life is the subject of a captivating biography by Robert Coram, *Boyd: The Fighter Who Changed the Art of War* (New York: Little, Brown, 2002.) Coram's book should be regarded as the source of all statements about Boyd's life in this book that are not otherwise attributed. Statements about Boyd's strategy and intentions are my personal recollection, unless separately referenced.

9   All of the other American services—and many foreign countries—possess elite units with exceptional fighting characteristics. The Marines, however, are the only service made up entirely of such units. It is essentially an all-elite force.

10   Basil H. Liddell Hart, *History of the Second World War*, echoed by German General F. W. von Mellenthin in *Panzer Battles*

11   Douglas Orgill, German Armor, *Ballentine's Illustrated History of the Violent Century, Weapons Book No. 41.*

12   Len Deighton, *Blitzkreig.*

13   Yes, the same Rommel that the British later nicknamed "The Desert Fox." His experiments with time as a weapon go back to his experiences as an infantry leader in the First World War.

14   Deighton, 232-233

15   Blumentritt, Gunther (General der Infanterie), "Experience Gained in the History of War on the Subject of Command Technique," 27 January 1947, quoted in Boyd, "Organic Design for Command and Control," May 1987.

16   Deighton, 234

17   B. H. Liddell Hart, *Strategy.*

18   J. F. C. Fuller, *The Conduct of War: 1789-1961: A Study of the Impact of the French, Industrial, and Russian Revolutions on War and Its Conduct.*

19   Stalk, George. "Time - The Next Source of Competitive Advantage." *Harvard Bus. Rev.*, Jul.-Aug. 1988.

Chapter II Visible Figures Alone

[20] William Scherkenbach, *The Deming Route to Quality and Productivity.* 44

[21] Perhaps the best book on time-based competition, per se, is George Stalk and Tom Hout, *Competing Against Time*, New York: Free Press, 1990. I have more recommendations in Chapter VII.

[22] In a real Pentagon model, effectiveness coefficients would most likely be given in 2 or three significant digits: .496 instead of .5, for example.

[23] In the real world, it does not follow that cheaper = less effective. Sometimes the simpler, more rugged, and more reliable weapon produces the best results on the battlefield.

[24] The F-15 has enjoyed an enviable combat record—no losses in air-to-air engagements. But tests in the late 1970s showed that the advantage due to the aircraft itself is more like 2 to 1 against pilots of equal skill in the mass, confused air battles like the Israelis fought against the Arabs and that we were expecting against the Soviets. Boyd, by the way, is considered a principle architect of the F-15 program—for details, see Coram's book. I was a junior participant in several of the meetings at the Pentagon where the Air Force presented these calculations.

[25] Norman Augustine, *Augustine's Laws*, New York: Viking, 1983. Recent cost overruns in America's two new fighter programs, the F/A-22 and F-35, suggest that Augustine may have been optimistic.

[26] Congress capped the procurement and R&D budgets for the F/A-22 in 1997. If costs continue to climb, either Congress will have to lift the cap, or the Air Force will receive fewer than 218 aircraft.

[27] There are ways to reduce costs in most industries while actually improving quality, which the Japanese automakers, for example, routinely achieve. These "lean production" methodologies can confer enormous competitive advantage, and they are actually examples of the same time-based strategies described in this book. I will discuss this further in Chapter VII.

[28] Lynn Montross, *Warfare Through the Ages.*

[29] It is magnificent, but it is not war. A similar observation could be made for GM's multi-billion investment in robotics during the 1980s or much of the merger and acquisition activity of the 1990s.

[30] Bruce Catton, *Never Call Retreat*, Garden City (NY): Doubleday, 1965, p. 145.

31 Samuel Griffith's introduction to his translation provides a most readable explanation of the foundations of Sun Tzu's strategy.

32 Hanshi Steve Kaufman trans., 66. Note that Musashi is referring to speed, and not time.

33 "On the Production of Victory: Empirical Determinants of Battlefield Success in Modern War," cited in Alan B. Krueger, "Trying To Predict A Military Victory," *New York Times*, February 6, 2003.

34 Major General F. W. von Mellenthin, *Panzer Battles*, University of Oklahoma Press, 1956. The quote is on page 349 of the 1971 Ballentine edition.

35 John K. Herr, *The Story of the U.S. Cavalry, 1775-1942*. There is a marker commemorating this event about three miles east of Cedar Bluff in northeastern Alabama. The Cherokee County (Alabama) web site has links to several stories about Streight's surrender.

36 UNIX and Mac OS X devotees may admit that their systems are vulnerable to "kernel panics." Although these may cause great distress and disruption to their users, kernel panics usually result not from bad strategy but from incompatible software or hardware.

37 James A. Polk, "The Criticality of Time in Combat," *Armor*, May-June 1988.

38 Only arrogance can explain why executives from such failed companies as Enron and MCI allegedly committed felonies.

Chapter III Sting Like a Bee

39 United States Central Command (USCENTCOM) Briefing Transcript for April 4, 2003, Doha, Qatar.

40 "Wars of the Future," *The Wall Street Journal*, Review and Outlook Section, February 4, 2003. To be fair to the *Journal*, *The Christian Science Monitor* carried a similar article on the same day.

41 As of this writing, there has not been a satisfactory explanation of the large short sales (speculating that the price of a stock would drop) of United Airlines stock just before 9/11. It is therefore entirely possible that al-Qa'ida made money from the attacks.

42 I am indebted for this observation to Professor Ross Gagliano, then of the Computer Science Department of Georgia State University in Atlanta, sometime around 1988.

43 A unit performing maneuver war might charge across no man's land, but such an action would probably form part of a larger scheme of maneuver. The unit could be launching a frontal attack, for example, to distract the enemy, while the rest of the unit tried to penetrate or turn a flank. Chapter VI, on surprise, will go into this further.

44 For a soldier's eye description of how this works on the battlefield today, read *Phantom Soldier* and *The Tiger's Way* by H. John Poole.

45 Martin van Creveld, *Fighting Power*, Greenwood Publishing, 1982. Although focused on military effectiveness, it could almost be entitled "Organizational Power," since it is really about creating organizations that can generate the high levels of energy and initiative needed to carry out Boyd-type strategies.

46 A comprehensive look at the use of these principles by the Israeli Defense Force, can be found in van Creveld's *The Sword and the Olive*. In *The Transformation of War* (1990) van Creveld describes how "terrorism" and other emerging forms of warfare use Boyd-like strategies. Boyd and van Creveld met and corresponded on several occasions.

47 Malone, Dandridge M., *Small Unit Leadership: A Commonsense Approach*, San Francisco: Presidio Press, 1995.

48 Fuller, op.cit., 73

49 Boulder, CO: Westview Press, 1985.

50 Griffith trans, 83

51 ibn Khaldun, *The Muqaddamah*, F. Rosenthal, *op. cit.*

52 From an interview with General Gaedke conducted by John Boyd and Pierre Sprey for Battelle Memorial Labs under contract with the Office of the Secretary of Defense in the early 1980s. Unfortunately, copies are not generally available.

53 Kenneth Macksey, *Panzer Division, Ballantine's Illustrated History of World War II, Weapons Book No. 21*.

54 Giap, General Vo Nguyen, *People's War People's Army*, Hanoi: Foreign Languages Publishing House, 1961. 123-124

55 Gaedcke interview with Boyd, 26

56 von Mellethin, op. cit.

57 The notion of "commander's intent" complements *Schwerpunkt*, but generally has a longer time focus. The *Schwerpunkt* may shift several times to accomplish the commander's intent.

58   Boyd, *Patterns of Conflict*

59   Musashi, *A Book of Five Rings.*

60   Liddell Hart, *German Generals Talk*

61   Fuller, op. cit. 114

62   Gaedke interview with Boyd, 38

63   *The Japanese Art of War*, 106.

64   Deighton, *Blitzkrieg*

65   Robert Coram used the term "acolyte" to describe six men whose careers were changed by their relationship with Boyd. His book contains biographical sketches of Pierre Sprey and the other acolytes.

66   Pierre Sprey, telcon, 4/13/90

67   There are several descriptions of how Boyd used EM to examine the MiG vs. the F-86. See for example Grant Hammond, *The Mind of War*, and Coram, *Boyd.*

68   "State" in air-to-air combat refers to the aircraft's airspeed, altitude, and direction at that specific time.

69   Giap, 161

70   Balck interview with Boyd, 2

71   The intelligence organizations are the Defense Intelligence Agency and the National Security Agency, both three-star billets. The Air Force agency is Air Force Materiel Command, commanded by a four-star. Intelligence is more valued by the civilians who run the Office of the Secretary of Defense, as demonstrated by the recent creation of the new Undersecretary of Defense for Intelligence (an "undersecretary" is the highest organizational level in the Pentagon, ranking just below the secretary and his/her deputy.)

72   From a new translation by the Denma Translation Group, Shambhala Press, 2001.

73   Boyd, telcon. 2/1990

74   From Boyd's final definition of "agility," presented at the 1989 DoD Agility Conference and related to the author by telephone conversation in 1990.

75   Related by Boyd in a telephone conversation in 1994 as a comment on an earlier version of this manuscript.

76   Keith Hammonds, "The Strategy of the Fighter Pilot," *Fast Company*, June 2002. An extremely well-written introduction to Boyd's ideas.

77   Since, for example, striking with too much speed can throw one off balance. See Hanshi Steve Kaufman's *The Martial Artist's Book of Five Rings*, Boston: Charles E. Tuttle, 1994. 35.

78   Sun Tzu, Griffith translation, 41.

79   Clausewitz, Graham trans. 164 in the Penguin Classics edition.

80   Recounted in Coram, *Boyd*, p. 425. I was sitting in a hotel room in Riyadh, less than a mile from where General Neal was speaking. I immediately tried calling Boyd, but the line was busy. Thanks to Coram, I now know it was probably Spinney.

81   Headquarters, Department of the Army, *Field Manual 3-0, Operations*, 14 June 2001 (replaces earlier Operations manuals which were numbered FM 100-5.) Available on-line.

82   There is some debate over how successful the Jedi Knights were in shaping Schwarzkopf's planning—see Coram, 424.

83   Air Force Manual 1-1. *Basic Aerospace Doctrine of the United States Air Force*. March 1984. This manual was revised and reissued in 1992 and 1997.

84   Coram, *op. cit.*

85   Hammond, Grant, *The Mind of War*, Washington: Smithsonian Institution, 2001. Hammond's biography tends more to Boyd's professional development, whereas Coram's is a biography in the traditional sense of telling the story of Boyd's life, including the evolution of his ideas. I recommend them both.

86   Marine Corps Doctrine Publication 1, *Warfighting*, HQ USMC, June 1997. This is a revision of the original version, entitled FMFM-1, *Warfighting*, March 1989. Both editions are available on-line as of this writing and the 1989 edition can often be found in bookstores.

87   Available in Coram's biography of Boyd.

88   *Annual Report to the President and to the Congress*, February 1992, page 121. I am indebted to Col G. I. Wilson, USMC (ret.) and one of the team who created *Warfighting*, for this quote.

89   Coram, 424.

Chapter IV What Strategy Is and What It Can Do for You

90   Weigley, Russell, *The American Way of War*, 18

91   Cleary trans. Zhang Yu, one of the canonical commentators on Sun Tzu, interpreting the passage at the end of Book 1 of *The Art of War*, "The one

with many strategic factors in his favor wins." Numbers and technology are not among the strategic factors. This is the full text of the excerpt that opens Chapter I of this book.

92   Greek strategic thought is well documented. My sources are Dr. Jonathan Shay's *Achilles in Vietnam* and *Odysseus in America*.

93   "I decline to accept the end of man … I believe that man will not merely endure: he will prevail." From Faulkner's Nobel Prize acceptance speech, Stockholm, December 10, 1950.

94   An inspiring story, but one without a happy ending. When the Crusaders finally entered Jerusalem, they proceeded to the Al Aqsa Mosque, where the Muslim population had gathered under a white flag, and slaughtered every man, woman, and child. When Saladin reconquered the city ninety years later, he could certainly have returned the favor. Instead, he accepted the Christians' surrender and personally guaranteed their safe passage out of the city. Even today, Muslim writers cite this incident as evidence of their moral superiority.

95   Boyd, *Patterns of Conflict*, 143.

96   I am writing this on a 600 MHz iBook (a Mac laptop.)

97   The term used by David Bradford & Allan Cohen in *Managing for Excellence: The Guide for Developing High Performance in Contemporary Organizations*, John Wiley & Sons, 1984.

98   Boyd, *Patterns of Conflict*, 143, 144.

99   "Best laid plans o' mice an' men gang aft agley," from "To A Mouse."

100   Boyd did not like arrows to represent plans. In the symbolic sense of "the arrow of time," however, which is pretty much how I am using it here, he did not object. In fact, he read and commented on at least three versions of this chapter before his death in 1997, and the one you are reading is very close to the last one he saw.

101   Boyd, "Strategic Game of ? and ?," June 1987, p. 58.

102   Edward Meade Earle, *The Making of Modern Strategy*. Astounding as it may seem, most of the military establishment had not received the message by the end of World War I, and were still throwing men and horses headlong against the new weapons of mass destruction.

103   The Marines were so impressed with this book that they invited Card to come to Quantico and discuss it with him.

[104] We used to say at Lockheed that fighter pilots wanted two things: a death ray and the control stick moved a half inch to the left.

[105] James Risen, "Why Can't America Catch Up?" *Los Angeles Times*, January 14, 1990.

[106] The Newton was perhaps the first commercially available personal digital assistant, a market segment later developed successfully by such companies as Palm, Handspring, and RIM (the Blackberry.)

[107] Following Polk, "The Criticality of Time in Combat"

[108] Joseph Juran, *Managerial Breakthrough*. New York: McGraw-Hill, 1964

[109] Stratford P. Sherman, "Inside the Mind of Jack Welch." *Fortune* 27 March 1989

[110] Tom Peters; *Fortune* April 9, 1990.

[111] Roger Schmenner "The Merit of Making Things Fast," *Sloan Mgmt. Rev.*, Fall 1988. This conclusion was most famously validated by MIT's International Motor Vehicle Project, which formed the basis for *The Machine That Changed the World*.

[112] Actually, some work-in-process (WIP) inventory is always required. It is buffer inventory, which cushions the effects of poor quality, that is "evil" and must be and can be eliminated. WIP inventory is managed by the *kanban* system, as an organic part of controlling production, and not by a separate inventory control system.

[113] This is the name Deming used in *Out of the Crisis*.

[114] Invited address to the Office of the Secretary of the Navy, February 2002, Washington DC (available at http:/www.belisarius.com)

Chapter V A Climate for Winning in Business

[115] Ibn Khaldun, *The Muqaddimah*, trans. Fritz Rosenthal, abridged and edited N. J. Dawood, London: Routledge and Kegan Paul, 1967.

[116] "The Key for Southwest: Remain Flexible," interview with Herb Kelleher, *Business Week*, February 3, 2003.

[117] One recent example: Robert Simons, Henry Mintzberg, and Kunal Basu, "Memo to CEOs," *Fast Company*, June 2002. The issue's cover read: "Memo to CEOs: Why Nobody Trusts You and What You Can Do About It."

[118] Shigeo Shingo, *Non-Stock Production*, 419

[119] Charles Handy, "Trust and the Virtual Organization," *Harvard Business Review*, May-June 1995.

[120] "Fair Process: Managing in the Knowledge Economy," W. Chan Kim and Renee Mauborg, *Harvard Business Review*, January 2003.

[121] Michael Popkin, *Active Parenting*, 46

[122] Robert Galford and Anne Seibold Drapeau, "The Enemies of Trust," *Harvard Bus. Rev.*, February 2003.

[123] Roger Penrose, *The Emperor's New Mind*

[124] Gary Klein, *Sources of Power*, MIT Press, 1998. This superb book belongs in every strategist's library. The follow-on, *Intuition at Work*, 2003, is also excellent. Both of these books document that implicit communications and *Fingerspitzengefühl* actually work.

[125] Boyd, "Organic Design," 23.

[126] Musashi, Kaufman trans., 94

[127] *muri*—unreasonableness, avoided by standardized work, flow, and time; *mura*—inconsistencies, avoided by just-in-time systems and pull; and *muda*—waste, eliminated by continuous improvement (kaizen). All three working in harmony form a continuously improving system.

[128] Musashi, Victor Harris trans. Cleary's *Japanese Art of War* elaborates further on this point.

[129] Bruce I. Gudmundsson, *Stormtroop Tactics, Innovation in the German Army, 1914-1918*, Westport (CT): Praeger, 1989. Don't let the esoteric title discourage you. This is a most readable study of cultural change that will help the leaders of any large organization.

[130] Risen, "Japan's", D6

[131] Marine Corps Doctrine Publication 6, *Command and Control*.

[132] Weick, K. E., "Managerial Thought in the Context of Action," in S. Srivastva (ed.), *The Executive Mind*, San Francisco: Jossey-Bass, 1983, quoted in Gary Klein, *Sources of Power*, 1998. I have revised the exact statement of Weick's recommendation to emphasize the contractual nature of the discussion.

[133] "Robert Noyce and his Congregation," *Forbes ASAP*, August 25, 1997, 103-106.

[134] Spencer E. Ante, "The New Blue," *Business Week*, March 17, 2003.

[135] Stalk & Hout, 58.

[136] Cypress fell victim to the general collapse of the technology sector, but survived and had a profitable Q3 2003 (profit before taxes $27.4 million.)

[137] Rodgers dismantled this system in 1992. Although, as he writes on the Cypress website, he still believes the fundamental idea was sound, he now concedes that a vice president who was late on 28% of his goals might actually have done a better job, and contributed more to the company, than one who only missed 3%.

[138] Alan Webber, "To Beat Japan, the U.S. Must Stop Making Excuses," *Atlanta Journal and Constitution*, August 6, 1989.

[139] James Ogilvy, "Living Without a Goal," *The Futurist*, May-June 1995, p. 10, quoted in *Information Week*, July 1995, p. 93.

[140] Ken Kreafle, vice president of quality for Toyota's Georgetown KY facility in Richard McCormick, Ed., *Lean Machines*. Annandale (VA): Publishers & Producers, 2002 (*http://www.manufacturingnews.com*)

[141] Toyota Motor Corporation, *Toyota Production System*, 1992.

[142] Allen Ward, et. al., "The Second Toyota Paradox: How Delaying Decisions Can Make Better Cars Faster," *Sloan Management Review*, Spring 1995. This is a classic study of applying the strategy underlying the Toyota Production System (and maneuver conflict in general) to the non-manufacturing arena. Not one of the techniques of the TPS make the transition, showing one more time why you can't simply cookie cutter the principles of the TPS into other areas. Most attempts to apply lean principles to functions such as finance or personnel are not going to produce useful results.

[143] Boyd, *Patterns of Conflict*, 78.

[144] For "exploratory marketing," Gary Hamal and C. K. Pralahad, "Corporate Imagination and Expeditionary Marketing," *Harvard Bus. Rev.*, July-August 1991.

[145] German doctrine did not give a name to the parts of the operation that were not the *Schwerpunkt*. Boyd did not speak German, and I am not sure where he got the term *Nebenpunkt*. Its meaning does fit with the idea of "secondary point."

[146] I am indebted to Col Mike Wyly, USMC (ret.), for his patient explanation of how these concepts actually work on the battlefield. I certainly take full responsibility, however, for any remaining errors.

[147] Andy Grove, former CEO of Intel recounts the details of this campaign in *Only the Paranoid Survive*.

[148] Boyd takes up this issue on pages 28 & 29 of "Organic Design for Command and Control." In particular, he recommends Martin van Creveld's "directed telescope," described in *Command in War* (1982.) This idea that observation changes the thing observed is familiar from physics as the Heinsenberg Uncertainty Principle. In organizational theory, it is sometimes called "Goodhart's Law," which, following Professor Marilyn Strathern, states: Once a measure becomes a goal or target, it ceases to be a valid measure. For more information, see: *http://www.atm.damtp.cam.ac.uk/people/mem/papers/LHCE/goodhart.html*

[149] Boyd, "Organic Design," 16.

[150] Allen Ward, et. al., *op. cit.*

[151] K. A. Ericsson, and Charness, N., "Expert Performance: Its Structure and Acquisition." American Psychologist, 49(8):725-747, cited in Klein, *Sources of Power*, 302.

[152] According to COL (Ret.) David Hackworth in *Steel My Soldiers' Hearts.*

[153] "In the Eye of the Storm," *Aviation Week*, March 1, 2004, p. 44. The magazine recommends that airlines focus on cost reductions and process improvements, replacing people with technology, and reducing quality in areas that customers "aren't willing to pay for." Such a mindset opens possibilities for airlines that can provide both improved quality *and* lower costs, analogous to the Japanese auto industry in the 1980s.

[154] Those familiar with Musashi will recognize my borrowing of his carpenter metaphor.

Chapter VI Surprise and Anticipation: The Real Principles of War, as Applied to Business

[155] "How Jack Welch Runs GE", *Business Week*, 8 June 1998.

[156] Griffith trans, 91

[157] Cleary translation, 95.

[158] Sir Arthur Conan Doyle, "Silver Blaze"

[159] Michael Page, *The Power of Ch'i*, p. 20

[160] Excellent descriptions of Alexander's campaigns and why this strategy worked against the Persians can be found in John Keegan's *Mask of Command*. Incidentally, this is why it is not correct to insist that one should always hurl strength against weakness, as you sometimes read in descriptions of

maneuver warfare. In fact, you should not always do anything, otherwise you become predictable.

[161] "Thinking Like Marines," available on *http://www.belisarius.com*.

[162] As a result, according to this story, we virtually stopped recruiting Soviet agents. Spy novelist and former journalist Robert Littell has written a very entertaining novel, *The Company*, developing the idea that the Russians had mastered this game of ambiguity and deception and were manipulating the Counterintelligence chief's paranoia.

[163] Boyd, *Patterns of Conflict*, 14

[164] *ibid*, 115

[165] *ibid*, 128

[166] *ibid*, 132

[167] *ibid*, 15

[168] Hal Clifford, "Six Sigma," *Continental*, November 1997, 64-67

[169] I've waited years to use this expression in describing the auto industry.

[170] Womack and Jones, *Lean Thinking*, Chapter 9.

[171] If Musashi's chance of winning any individual fight were 97%, his odds of surviving all 60 would only amount to 16%. His strategy was framed not in terms of increasing odds, since he didn't want to leave his survival to any degree of chance at all, but of ways to arrange a sure thing. Similarly, Sun Tzu insisted in many passages that it was possible to make oneself invincible.

[172] Hanshi Steve Kaufmann translation, *The Martial Artist's Book of Five Rings*. This was Boyd's favorite translation.

[173] Following Tom Peters, again, who once noted that the real business of any company is conducted around the water cooler and coffee pot. As an aside, this can be a challenge if you've outsourced large chunks of your company to another continent.

[174] Cleary, *The Japanese Art of War*

[175] Power tends to corrupt and absolute power corrupts absolutely (author's note: that is, there is no doubt about it.)

[176] You might also refer to Colonel Douglas MacGregor, "Initiative in Battle: Past and Future," *Marine Corps Gazette*, August 1997, and Mike Wyly's "Thinking Like Marines" at *http://www.belisarius.com*.

Chapter VII What You Really Do with OODA Loops

177 Patton gave a series of rousing speeches to the troops of the Third Army before they deployed to France. George C. Scott's monologue at the start of the movie *Patton* follows those speeches as closely as propriety would allow. This excerpt is from the version at: *http://www.pattonhq.com/speech.html.*

178 Boyd, *Patterns of Conflict*, 132

179 It follows, as Wolfram notes, that simplicity—straight lines and perfect circles, for example—and not complexity would be evidence for divine intervention in the universe. Alas, these are rarely found in nature, and where they are (e.g., the *nearly* spherical shape of celestial bodies) they can be easily explained by natural processes. This is not an argument for atheism, but merely a statement that the wondrous complexity of nature is exactly what we'd expect from a universe generated by simple machines operating over a long period of time. The same is true of human organizations—complexity is the natural order of things; simplicity requires intelligence and experimentation, that is, hard work.

180 Delta Express and Shuttle by United. It is too early to tell whether their new offerings, Song and Ted, respectively, will succeed. One thing is certain, however. Even if successful, they will do nothing to change the cultures or profitability of the legacy portions of their companies.

181 Taiichi Ohno, *Toyota Production System*, Portland, Oregon: Productivity Press, 1988. The Japanese original was published in 1978. Taiichi Ohno died in 1990.

182 These results were documented in the book, *The Machine That Changed the World.*

183 *http://www.marines.com.* If you could get in, it would be the best management education you'll ever receive.

184 Kaufman trans., 60.

185 Col Wyly is the founder and executive director of the Bossov Ballet Theater, in residence at the Maine Central Institute in Pittsfield, Maine. He reports that his experience as both a student and a practitioner of maneuver warfare serve him well in this position. "Thinking Like Marines" can be found at *http://www.belisarius.com.*

Printed in the United States
117003LV00003B/172-177/A